PEREGRINE BOOKS

PATTERNS IN NATURE

In a stunning synthesis of art and science, Peter Stevens explains the universal patterns in which nature expresses herself. He provides a fresh way of viewing and understanding the physical world.

'When we see how the branching of trees resembles the branching of arteries and the branching of rivers, how crystal grains look like soap bubbles and the plates of a tortoise's shell, how the fiddleheads of ferns, stellar galaxies, and water emptying from the bathtub spiral in a similar manner, then we cannot help but wonder why nature uses only a few kindred forms in so many contexts. . . It turns out that those patterns and forms are peculiarly restricted, that the immense variety that nature creates emerges from the working and reworking of only a few formal themes.'

With his elegant and lucid prose, illuminated by hundreds of photographs and geometrical drawings, the author examines those themes and explains how they evolve according to the laws of stress, flow, turbulence, least effort, surface tension, close packing, and, most important, the constraints of three-dimensional space.

Peter S. Stevens is Director of the Architectural Planning Office for the Harvard Medical Area and is also a painter and photographer. *Patterns in Nature* was funded by a Guggenheim Fellowship while Mr Stevens was a lecturer in Visual and Environmental Studies at the Carpenter Visual Arts Center at Harvard University.

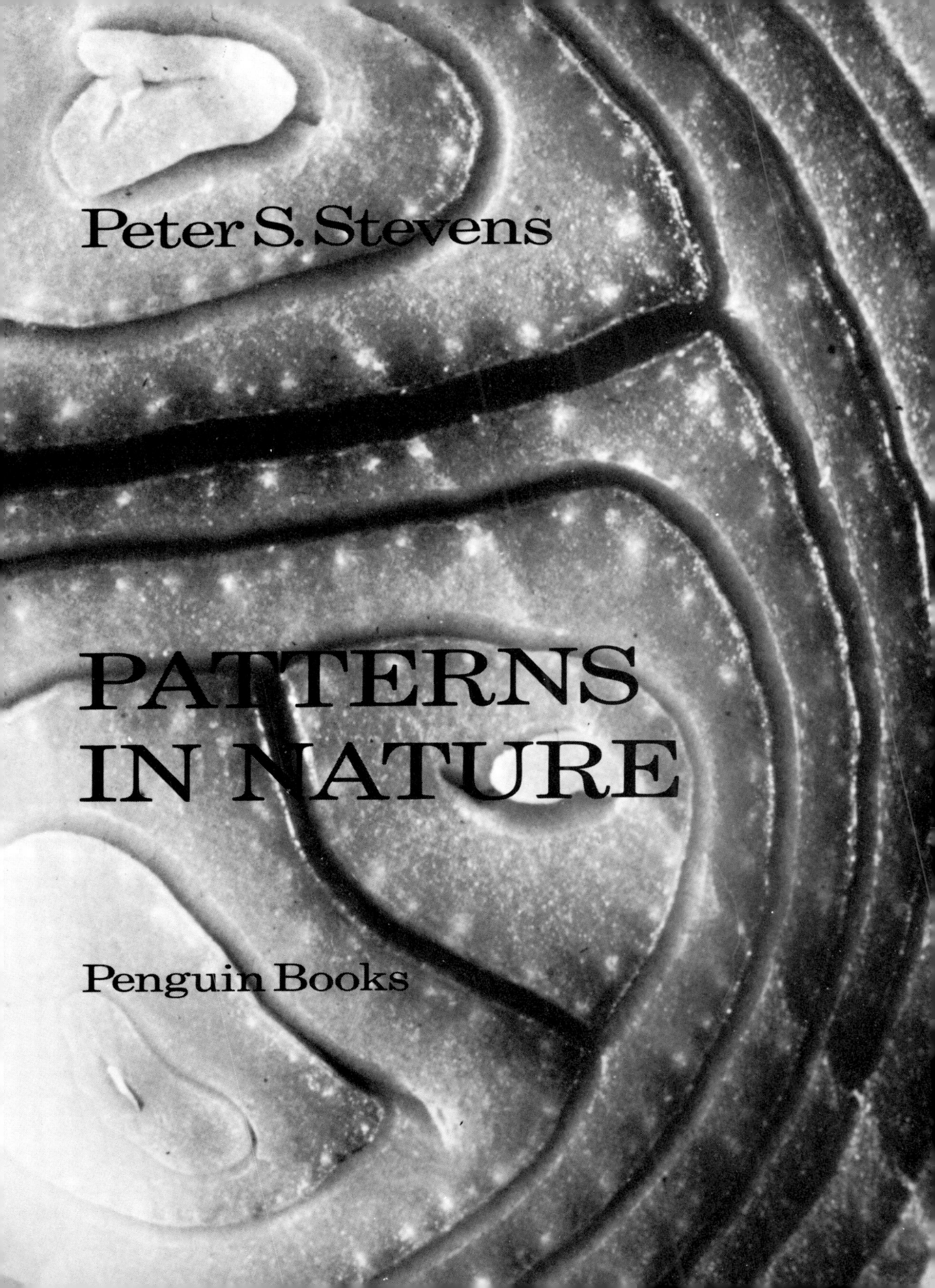

Peter S. Stevens

PATTERNS
IN NATURE

Penguin Books

Penguin Books Ltd, Harmondsworth, Middlesex, England
Penguin Books, 625 Madison Avenue, New York, New York 10022, U.S.A.
Penguin Books Australia Ltd, Ringwood, Victoria, Australia
Penguin Books Canada Ltd, 2801 John Street, Markham, Ontario, Canada L3R 1B4
Penguin Books (N.Z.) Ltd, 182–190 Wairau Road, Auckland 10, New Zealand

—

First published in the U.S.A. by Little, Brown & Co. 1974
Published in Peregrine Books 1976
Reprinted 1977

—

—

Made and printed in Great Britain by
Butler & Tanner Ltd,
Frome and London

To Joyce, David, Karl, and Jean

Acknowledgments

Two GENEROSITIES made this book possible — the John Simon Guggenheim Memorial Foundation granted me a fellowship, and Eduard Sekler provided me with a place to work at the Carpenter Center amid the activities of Harvard's Department of Visual and Environmental Studies.

I am deeply indebted to my father, S. S. Stevens, who reviewed the entire manuscript. He has not lived to see the finished work, but his interest sustained its development. I am also indebted to Rudolf Arnheim for his careful reading and thoughtful comments and to Arthur Loeb for his suggestions.

The discussions of a small group of teachers and students, the Philomorphs, who met at Harvard to pursue the study of form, were a stimulus to the book. In addition to Arnheim and Loeb, the group boasted as regular members Michael Woldenberg, Stephen Gould, Ranko Bon and, from the Massachusetts Institute of Technology, Cyril Smith.

I wish to thank Didi Stevens who saw to it that the manuscript was typed, edited, and ready for publication and Esther S. Yntema who brought the work to final fruition.

Contents

1

Space and Size

And this our life, exempt from public haunt,
Finds tongues in trees, books in the running brooks,
Sermons in stones, and good in everything.

— SHAKESPEARE,
As You Like It, Act II, Sc. 1

OUR SUBJECT concerns the visual patterns and forms in the natural world. It turns out that those patterns and forms are peculiarly restricted, that the immense variety that nature creates emerges from the working and reworking of only a few formal themes. Those limitations on nature bring harmony and beauty to the natural world.

It may seem curious to dwell on nature's limitations when a glance out the window reveals such overwhelming diversity. Clouds and chickadees, galaxies and grasshoppers, eels and elms: one cannot help but be impressed with nature's variety. Even among things that seem superficially the same, like snowflakes, or leaves from the same tree, each differs in subtle ways from its fellows.

But then when we see how the branching of trees resembles the branching of arteries and the branching of rivers, how crystal grains look like soap bubbles and the plates of a tortoise's shell, how the fiddleheads of ferns, stellar galaxies, and water emptying from the bathtub spiral in a similar manner, then we cannot help but wonder why nature uses only a few kindred forms in so many different contexts. Why do meandering snakes, meandering rivers, and loops of string adopt the same pattern, and why do cracks in mud and markings on a giraffe arrange themselves like films in a froth of bubbles?

In matters of visual form we sense that nature plays favorites. Among her darlings are spirals, meanders, branching patterns, and 120-degree joints. Those patterns occur again and again. Nature acts like a theatrical producer who brings on the same players each night in different costumes for different roles. The players perform a limited repertoire: pentagons make most of the flowers but none of the crystals; hexagons handle most of the repetitive two-dimensional patterns but never by themselves enclose three-dimensional space. On the other hand, the spiral is the height of versatility, playing roles in the replication of the smallest virus and in the arrangement of matter in the largest galaxy.

A look behind the footlights reveals that nature has no choice in the assignment of roles to players. Her productions are shoestring operations, encumbered by the constraints of three-dimensional space, the necessary relations among the sizes of things, and an eccentric sense of frugality. In the space at nature's command, five regular polyhedrons can be produced, but no more. Seven systems of crystals can be employed, but never an eighth. Absolute size decrees that the lion will never fly nor the robin roar. Every part of every action must abide by the rules.

The Nature of Space

Nothing puzzles me more than time and space; and yet nothing troubles me less, as I never think about them.
—CHARLES LAMB

OF ALL THE CONSTRAINTS ON NATURE, the most far-reaching are imposed by space. For space itself has a structure that influences the shape of every existing thing.

The idea that space has structure may sound strange, since we usually think of space as a kind of nothingness that is the absence of structure. We think of space as the emptiness within an empty container, as the passive backdrop for the lively play of all material things.

It turns out, however, that the backdrop, the all-pervading nothingness, is not so passive. The nothingness has an architecture that makes real demands on things. Every form, every pattern, every existing thing pays a price for its existence by conforming to the structural dictates of space.

Our ignorance about the effects of space parallels the ignorance of fish about the effects of water. And just as fish would understand their environment better through studies of buoyancy, pressure, and streamlining in different liquids, so we have come to understand our own environment better through studies of transformation, extension, and curvature in different spaces. We did not recognize the special character of our space until the non-Euclidean geometers of the nineteenth century and Einstein in the twentieth century showed that there are other spaces, and that patterns and forms in those other spaces differ from the ones we see in ours. Since our brains and perceptual processes have evolved to suit our own space, we cannot visualize those other spaces, but we have devised self-consistent mathematical descriptions of them, and we have come to recognize that the spaces in the world of the very small, in the world of the fundamental particles, and in the world of the very large, at the scale of the universe as a whole, differ dramatically from the space in which we live.

What kind of stuff makes space and precisely how it affects the shape of things are pressing questions in modern physics. At the turn of the century Mendeleev, who discovered the periodicity of the elements, posed the idea that space consists of particles a million times smaller than the hydrogen atom, and that combinations of those particles produce atoms. That was a strange speculation. Mendeleev, you see, did not say that space was *filled* with little particles but that it *was* little particles. P. A. M. Dirac, John A. Wheeler, and other physicists have developed Mendeleev's idea and have likened space to a perhaps infinite array of tiny grains or a froth of bubbles. Perhaps, somehow, the shifting of those grains or bubbles produces the fundamental particles that form the basis for all material structures.

More and more in physics, the idea seems to be taking hold that space has real material structure. That thought shocks most of us. Space is no longer considered a passive background like a set of coordinates; it is thought to be a real agent that gives rise to all the rest of the material world. It is the primeval stuff from which all else springs. Thus our common-sense idea that space is a big nothing has been replaced with the more sophisticated thought that space is a big everything. Wheeler nicely summed up Einstein's conception of the modern view:

> Einstein, above his work and writing, held a long-term vision: There is nothing in the world except curved empty space. Geometry bent one way here describes gravitation. Rippled another way somewhere else it manifests all the qualities of an electromagnetic wave. Excited at still another place, the magic material that is space shows itself as a particle. There is nothing that is foreign and "physical" immersed in space.

And again

> There is nothing in the world except empty curved space. Matter, charge, electromagnetism, and other fields are only manifestations of the bending of space.

Wheeler goes still further. He supposes that the space of our universe is only one of an infinite number of spaces, that our space is only a single point in Superspace, which is the totality of all spatial possibilities. And if and when the universe, after its present expansion, contracts and then expands again for another round, it will most probably have a different spatial character, and since the one follows the other, it will contain very different forms.

So the puzzle of space that Charles Lamb chose not to think about lies at the heart of the problems faced by contemporary physics. We will leave the exploration of that puzzle to the physicists, and, rather than delve deeper into things unseen, we will stay with the visible world, for even there we discover ourselves controlled by the properties of space.

Curvature

"... And nature must obey necessity."
—SHAKESPEARE,
Julius Caesar, Act IV, Sc.3

SPACE IS UNIFORMLY SPREAD OUT. It is the same here and there as everywhere else. We become aware of how that spreading of space affects shape when we play with a piece of modeling clay.

Suppose you make a small disk of clay like that in the first frame of Figure 1. It is obvious that with a rolling pin you can spread the clay into a larger disk. Under the action of the rolling pin, the clay spreads evenly in all directions — just like the space in which it lies.

Now, suppose you press or flatten only the center of the disk. You can do that by manipulating the clay with your fingers. Flattening the center causes the center to spread and grow faster than the perimeter, and the disk naturally takes the shape of a bowl, as shown in the second frame.

You can also squeeze the perimeter of the disk so that it grows faster than the center. Again the disk will not lie flat. Instead, it thrusts itself simultaneously both forward and back to make a saddle. The saddle comes about just as naturally as the bowl. The clay is not molded into those forms but the forms arise naturally, depending upon where you press the clay. From playing with the clay, we are led to the discovery of a fundamental rule: if the center and perimeter both grow at the same rate, the material spreads in a plane; if the center grows faster than the perimeter, or the perimeter grows faster than the center, a bowl or a saddle results.

Here is another manifestation of the same principle.

1

a *b* *c*

d *e* *f*

When you play with equilateral triangles, you find that you can arrange six triangles neatly around a central point so that all the triangles lie flat, as shown again in Figure 1. Five triangles around a central point, however, take the form of a tent or an inverted bowl (frame *e*). And seven triangles around a point make an undulating saddle (frame *f*). The result is the same as for the clay: varying the extension of the perimeter with respect to the center transforms planes into bowls and saddles.

The reason for those transformations lies in the nature of space. The transformations have nothing to do with our intentions to make one form or another. No matter how we try, we cannot make a saddle from five equilateral triangles or a simple cup from seven.

Nature too is similarly constrained. She makes cups and saddles not as she pleases but as she must, as the distribution of material dictates. Observe the shell in Figure 2, for example. Since the perimeter of the shell grows at a faster rate than the center, the perimeter curls and wrinkles. No genes carry an image of how to place the wrinkles; no genes remember the shape of the shell; they only permit or encourage faster growth at the perimeter than at the center.

2

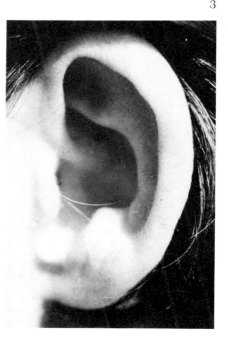

3

Similar differences of growth lead to the development of more complicated structures, like the outer shell of the human ear, shown in Figure 3. The convolutions of the outer ear arise like the convolutions in a piece of paper that has been sprinkled with water. The living tissue and the paper both bend and warp in accord with the differential expansion of their surfaces.

The cups and saddles tell us even more about the nature of space. Suppose we wish to make the cup lie flat. We can do either of two things: we can stretch the perimeter of the cup so that it expands as much as the center, or we can tear the perimeter to make serrated pieces that can be forced to lie flat. That stretching or tearing, or both together, illustrate the age-old difficulty of drawing a map of the spherical earth on a flat sheet of paper. The surface of the earth must be distorted or torn (Figure 4). The reason we cannot map the earth on a piece of paper is that forms are more closely bunched around the perimeter of a given area when they are distributed on a sphere than when they are distributed on a plane: the perimeter of a spherical area is too tight to lie flat. If the surface of the earth were shaped like a saddle, we would face the opposite problem. When we force a saddle to lie in a plane, the perimeter curls and folds because it is too loose.

4

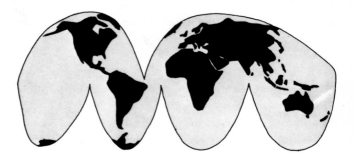

What we observe in those examples is that differential growth determines the shape or the curvature of a surface. We can directly observe the effects of differences in growth for two-dimensional surfaces because we can see those surfaces embedded in or surrounded by three-dimensional space. The principle by which differences in growth produce curvature applies to three-dimensional space as well. But to see the curvature of three-dimensional space, we would have to see it embedded in four-dimensional space. Unfortunately, that visualization is beyond our perceptual capacity.

Mathematically, however, we can describe curvature of three-dimensional space very well. We can even describe curvatures of four-dimensional space-time. For example, Einstein conceived that the universe has a four-dimensional space-time curvature that is something like the curvature of a sphere. Other conceptions see the universe as shaped like a saddle. Either way, the structure of space and the makeup of the visible world are indivisibly united.

Polyhedrons and Mosaics

THE MAKING OF AN OPEN CUP from five equilateral triangles poses an interesting question. If you continue to add triangles to the rim, will the cup wrap back on itself to make a complete enclosure? The answer is yes. Fifteen additional triangles, joined five at a time at the corners, will automatically make a closed container — a regular polyhedron with twenty triangular faces. It is pictured in the top right-hand frame of Figure 5. When you make that polyhedron, you cannot help but be impressed by the way all the triangles fall into place. They fit perfectly. You do not have to trim any edges, deform any corners, or force the fit in any way. Such a polyhedron is beautifully unequivocal; it either comes out perfectly or not at all. The conditions for its existence have been determined since the world began.

In addition to joining triangles five at a time, you can join them three at a time and four at a time to get a four-sided tetrahedron and an eight-sided octahedron. Similarly, too, you can join squares three at a time to get a cube, and regular five-sided pentagons three at a time to get a dodecahedron. Altogether, you can make five regular convex polyhedrons. They are pictured in Figure 5. Each of them has regular faces and regular corners. They were known to the ancient Greeks and from that day to this no one has added to their number. And no one ever will. No one will ever

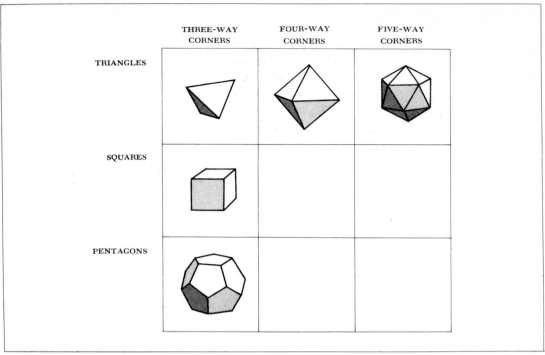

	THREE-WAY CORNERS	FOUR-WAY CORNERS	FIVE-WAY CORNERS
TRIANGLES			
SQUARES			
PENTAGONS			

5

6

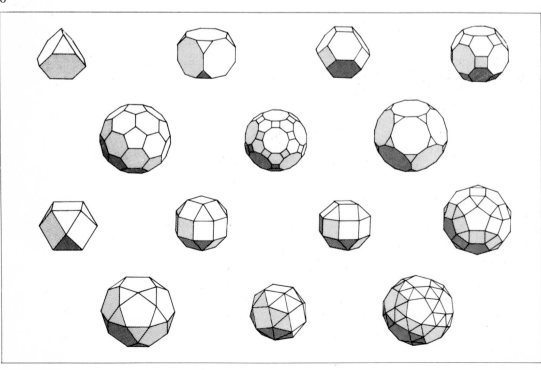

make a regular enclosure out of six-, seven-, or eight-sided polygons, or out of any other regular plane figures. Space allows the construction of only the five regular forms. As shown in the figure, three of the forms have lines that meet three at a time to make three-way corners, while one form has four-way and one form five-way corners. None have corners at which more than five elements join. None have faces with more than five edges.

By joining regular plane figures of more than one type, while keeping the corners or vertexes the same, you can, of course, make other polyhedrons, the semi-regular ones. But here again, the possibilities are limited. Excluding prisms, you can make only the fourteen semiregular polyhedrons shown in Figure 6. No more will be discovered.

Here are some of the limitations on those polyhedrons. Every form has three-, four-, or five-way corners, and every form has some faces with three, four, or five edges. If triangles or hexagons occur, they come in multiples of four: they number either four, eight, twenty, thirty-two, or eighty. Squares and octagons come in multiples of six: they number six, twelve, eighteen, or thirty. If pentagons or decagons occur there must be twelve of them. No form has faces with seven, nine, eleven, or a higher number of edges.

Further limitations on how elements can join show up when we combine the regular and semiregular polyhedrons to fill space without leaving gaps or holes. Including combinations that use regular prisms (a form that has a regular polygonal top and bottom joined by a belt of squares), we find only twenty-two space-filling clusters. Only polyhedrons with some triangular or square faces can join in such combinations. Polyhedrons with pentagonal faces cannot be used. A portion of one of those clusters is shown in Figure 7. It is a group of truncated octahedrons which picture the molecular geometry of the aluminosilicates and the statistically "ideal" soap froth which we will investigate further.

Analogous to the limited number of regular and

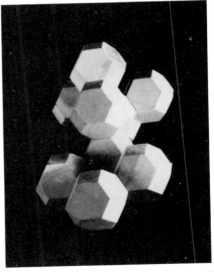

7

semiregular three-dimensional polyhedrons is the limited number of regular and semiregular two-dimensional mosaics. A portion of one of those mosaics was shown in the group of six equilateral triangles of Figure 1 (*d*). The triangles lie flat and if we add more triangles, still keeping six around each point, we can extend the array as much as we please in any direction. A little experimentation reveals the existence of only two other mosaics that have regular and identical pieces and that can be extended indefinitely. All three mosaics are pictured in Figure 8. We also find eight and only eight semiregular mosaics that combine regular polygons of more than one type while maintaining identical joints. They are pictured in Figure 9. Each of those mosaics combines triangles or squares or both together. Only three-, four-, or five-way joints are allowed.

Note the absence of pentagons in the groups of regular and semiregular mosaics. Pentagons do not combine with themselves or with other regular figures to fill space. Polyhedrons that have pentagonal faces also do not combine with one another to fill space. Thus we find that crystals, which are repetitive assemblages of molecules, never have regular five-sided faces. In fact, no inanimate form exhibits pentagonal symmetry. No regularly pentagonal snowflake has ever fallen from the sky. Only animate forms, complicated forms, structures beyond the interminable stacking of identical molecules, have shapes with five equal sides.

The regular and semiregular mosaics and polyhedrons provide the most explicit demonstration that nature's forms are limited. Seldom, however, must nature create such perfectly regular shapes. Seldom is she constrained to work with equilateral triangles or to make forms with identical corners. More often she can introduce variations. She can push and pull and add and take away. But in all her manipulations, she must bend and warp in accord with the amount of material at hand. Her planes, bowls, and saddles may not extend to infinity, make perfect polyhedrons, or curve with absolute precision, but they must lie flat, bend around on themselves, and undulate forward and

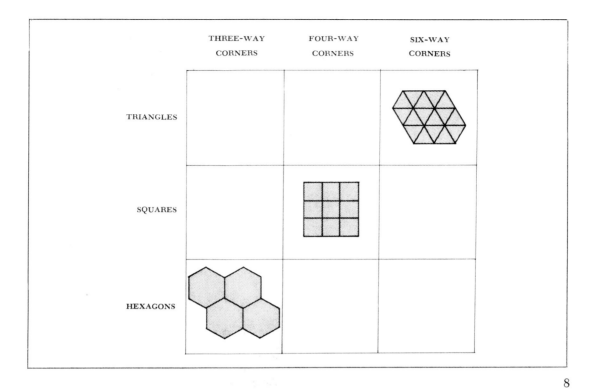

	THREE-WAY CORNERS	FOUR-WAY CORNERS	SIX-WAY CORNERS
TRIANGLES			
SQUARES			
HEXAGONS			

THREE-WAY CORNERS

FOUR-WAY CORNERS

FIVE-WAY CORNERS

back, in keeping with the limited ways in which material can be distributed in space.

The Effect of Scale

From what has already been demonstrated, you can plainly see the impossibility of increasing the size of structures to vast dimensions either in art or in nature; likewise the impossibility of building ships, palaces, or temples of enormous size in such a way that their oars, yards, beams, iron-bolts, and, in short, all their other parts will hold together; nor can nature produce trees of extraordinary size because the branches would break down under their own weight; so also it would be impossible to build up the bony structures of men, horses, or other animals so as to hold together and perform their normal functions if these animals were to be increased enormously in height; for this increase in height can be accomplished only by employing a material which is harder and stronger than usual, or by enlarging the size of the bones, thus changing their shape until the form and appearance of the animals suggest a monstrosity.

—Galileo

THE EFFECT OF MAGNITUDE or absolute size as a determinant of form shows again how space shapes the things around us. In studying polyhedrons we are unconcerned with magnitude. We assume that a cube is a cube no matter what its size. We find, however, that the geometric relations that arise from a difference in size affect structural behavior, and that a large cube is relatively weaker than a small cube. We also find, as a corollary, that in order to maintain the same structural characteristics a difference in size must be accompanied by a difference in shape.

To understand the effects of size and how they are derived from the spreading of space, consider again the regular polyhedrons pictured in Figure 5. The following table shows the surface areas and volumes of those solids, based on a dimension d taken to be the length of an edge. The tetrahedron, octahedron, and icosahedron are the solids with four, eight, and twenty triangular faces; the cube and dodecahedron have six square and twelve pentagonal faces.

PROPERTIES OF THE REGULAR POLYHEDRONS

	Area	Volume
Tetrahedron	$1.7321\ d^2$	$0.1178\ d^3$
Octahedron	$3.4641\ d^2$	$0.4714\ d^3$
Icosahedron	$8.6603\ d^2$	$2.1817\ d^3$
Cube	$6.0000\ d^2$	$1.0000\ d^3$
Dodecahedron	$20.6458\ d^2$	$7.6632\ d^3$

The table shows that the surface area of each solid is some number times d^2, whereas the volume of each solid is some number times d^3. The number preceding the term d^2 or d^3 is different for the five different solids. It happens as well that the numbers would be different if the curvature of space was different. But the general rules, which are true for all spaces of constant curvature, are that surface area is proportional to d^2, i.e., to the square of the linear dimension, whereas volume is proportional to d^3, the cube of the linear dimension.

The rules give us a measure of how space spreads. And thus they describe the outward spread of anything that distributes itself in space. Consider, for example, the spread of energy.

The energy flowing through each unit area diminishes with the square of the distance from the source. Thus the light grows dimmer, the sound softer, and the gravitational, magnetic, and electrical fields weaker the farther from the source you place your eye, ear, weighing scale, magnetometer, or potentiometer. Measuring the propagation of energy is similar to measuring the expanding surface of a balloon. When you measure close to the energy source, you measure a compact halo of energy that is like the constricted surface of a small balloon. The energy is dense and the signal is loud and clear. When you measure far from the source, you measure an expanded halo that is like the expanded surface of an inflated balloon. The energy is spread and dissipated. The same amount of energy, or elastic surface, surrounds the source at every distance from the source, but the density of the energy, or the surface, diminishes with increasing distance.

Putting the matter more directly, the inverse square law, the statement that energy diminishes, or varies inversely, as the square of its distance from the source, is not so much a description of energy as it is of the spatial arena in which the energy advances. The occurrence of the term d^2 in formulas for the propagation of light, sound, gravitational and electromagnetic fields is synonymous with the occurrence of d^2 in our table. It is an area term; it describes the size of the spherical surface around an energy source.

In the same way that many phenomena vary in proportion to surface, to d^2, many others vary in proportion to volume, to d^3. Chief among the properties dependent upon volume is weight. Little things are light, big things heavy. A fly is so light it can cling to the ceiling, like a piece of dust. The prowess of the fly is not so much a function of its sticky feet as of its small size. In fact, the point has been justly made that man too could walk on the ceiling, if he were small enough. And flight would pose no problem either. At the size of a fly, man's concern would rather be to stay on the ground. As J. B. S. Haldane observed, weight, or the pull of gravity, presents no problem to an animal even the size of a mouse:

> You can drop a mouse down a thousand-yard mine shaft; and, on arriving at the bottom, it gets a slight shock and walks away. A rat would probably be killed, though it can fall safely from the eleventh story of a building; a man is killed, a horse splashes.

A beached whale does not even have to fall to die; it can suffocate under its own weight stranded in shallow water.

We infer from our table of surfaces and volumes that as an object increases in size, its area and volume increase at strikingly different rates, the one as d^2 the other as d^3. The next table shows the significance of that difference.

HOW VOLUME INCREASES FASTER THAN AREA

Linear Dimension d	Area $\propto d^2$	Volume $\propto d^3$
1	1	1
2	4	8
4	16	64
8	64	512
16	256	4,096
32	1,024	32,768

An object with a linear dimension 32 times that of another has 1,024 times as much surface area and a staggering 32,768 times as much volume. A large object, therefore, has more volume in relation to its surface than a small object. In living forms, a large organism weighs more, as we have seen, and generates more heat than a small one. Those functions depend on the volume or mass of its tissues. The large organism is also weaker and has more difficulty dissipating heat and assimilating food and oxygen. Those functions depend on its surface area.

If the large organism is to function like its small cousin, it must compensate for its preponderance of volume by selectively increasing its critical surfaces. The general method of increasing surface area is to introduce complications: to flatten, grow hairs, branch, wrinkle, elongate, and hollow out. We see examples of those adaptations all about us.

In Figure 10, a young shoot extends flat leaves to the sun. As growth continues, the stem will branch

and put out more leaves, and then finally thicken, into a tough bough to carry still more leaves and branches. The proliferation of branches and leaves will enable the large spray to function like the small shoot.

In Figure 11 the stem of the celandine flattens into webs and leaves (*a*), and the enclosing sheath of the cornstalk folds outward into a long blade (*b*). We see that the celandine (*c*), as well as the grass (*d*), grows hairs, which, like thorns, cilia, fur, antennae, spines, and all the other prickly appendages of living things, keep surface commensurate with volume.

Networks of branches and roots increase surface area still further. According to Howard J. Dittmer at the University of Iowa, in only four months a single plant of rye grows 387 miles of root. When the root hairs are included, the length is 7,000 miles. Furthermore, large plants branch proportionately more than small ones. By way of example, Figure 12 shows the sprouting pod of the red mangrove with its few simple leaves and unbranched stem, in comparison with a thicket of mature trees. To keep their surface commensurate with their greatly increased volume, the large trees branch prolifically and put out a multitude of leaves. All their branching enables them to function like the little sprout. All their branching comes about because they have increased in size.

In Figure 13 increase in surface area is exemplified by branching. Shown there are the blood and air pathways of the human lung revealed by a latex casting (*a*), a mangrove thicket (*b*), arteries of a dog, again revealed in latex (*c*), and the bloom of the common smoke tree, *Cotinus coggygria* (*d*).

The branching of the circulatory systems in the human lung and in the dog are especially interesting as attempts to increase surface area. A small single-celled organism has no need for such complications. It does not require lungs or hearts or any system of circulation. It can breathe and absorb food directly through its cell wall, there being relatively more wall than interior tissue. When the single-celled organism grows, or when almost any cell grows for that matter,

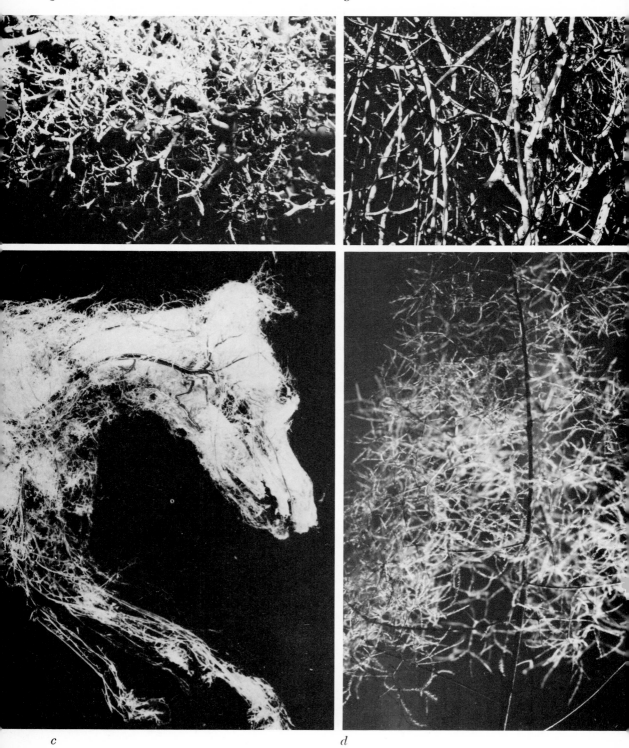

c

d

and the functions that depend upon surface can no longer sustain the inner tissue, the organism does not develop wrinkles, veins, or branches; it simply divides. It makes itself small again and starts over with a double identity and a comparatively greater surface for each of its parts. Thus we are not surprised to learn that cells exist within a limited range of size. They can be neither too big nor too small. Otherwise the functions dependent upon surface would not match those dependent upon volume.

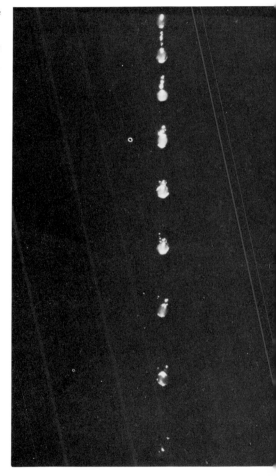

A nice analogy to cell division is shown in Figure 14, in which a small stream of water has been "stopped" with a stroboscopic light to reveal its constituent drops. The tension in the skin of a drop can enclose only so much liquid. If the volume of water is too great the little skin will burst. The volume must remain commensurate with the strength of the surface. And thus, as with cells, we find an upper limit of size. No drops are as big as baseballs or watermelons.

The point that things are restricted in size is, of course, the fundamental lesson. Different things are confined to different latitudes of dimension. Nucleons bind together to make nuclei of relatively fixed size, electrons join nuclei to make atoms of a well-defined magnitude, atoms unite to form molecules, molecules combine to make cells, and cells make organisms. You never find a nucleus, an atom, a molecule, or a cell as big as a man. Each form has its own dimensional realm, its upper and lower bounds. But each form combines and works together with others like itself to make larger structures and organizations.

Even within a given class of form, the properties of the small differ from those of the large. And, at least in the animal kingdom, those properties vary in a uniform and predictable manner. Small creatures breathe faster than large creatures. Their hearts beat faster, their voices are higher, and their wings or limbs move more rapidly. They consume more food in relation to their body weight, reproduce faster, and have shorter lifetimes.

As D'Arcy Thompson pointed out, the reason for

those variations is that the small muscle, be it heart, lung, wing, or vocal cord, oscillates faster than the large muscle, just as a short thin string, when it is plucked, vibrates more rapidly than a long thick one. We see the principle confirmed when we tabulate heartbeats of different animals:

HEARTBEATS

Least shrew	700 beats per minute
House cat	120
Man	72
Elephant	35–40
Whale	15–20

Since respiration is coupled with heartbeat — usually one breath is taken for every four heartbeats — the rate of breathing also decreases with increasing size. And so do wingbeats and the movement of limbs.

WINGBEATS

Midge	1,046 times per second
Mosquito	587
Honeybee	230
Hummingbird	100
Sparrow	15
Stork	2–3
Condor	0

Apparently, the small creature lives on a shorter time scale than the large. Its life passes more quickly. With twenty-five million heartbeats per life as the rule of thumb, we find that the rat lives for only three years, the rabbit seven, man seventy, and the elephant and whale even longer. By the same token, the small creature reproduces faster than the large — in a mere twenty minutes for some of the smallest bacteria.

We come to realize that both the small and the large have their advantages. The small creature has an edge over the large because it eats less food, in absolute amounts, because it is less complex and therefore harder to kill, and because with its high rate of reproduction it can easily breed its way out of environmental difficulty. A queen termite, for example, lays over eighty thousand eggs in a day, and in the time a single human embryo develops, a codling moth can produce over four hundred trillion descendants.

On the other side of the ledger, the larger animal is favored because it loses less heat through its relatively reduced surface. Thus it survives better in cold climates. In terms of its own body weight, the large animal consumes less food. A man, for example, eats one-fiftieth of his weight in three daily meals, whereas the pigmy shrew, which weighs less than a dime, eats continuously and devours several times its weight in a day. The large animal is a superior predator — especially man, who is big enough to wield a club effectively. Yet a man is not so big that he breaks his own bones when he falls. The large creature has more cells with which to make a brain and it has, as well, a longer life in which to use that brain. Man, with his remarkable brain, developed the use of fire, but, even apart from considerations of brain power, as F. W. Went has pointed out, only a creature of man's size could effectively control that fire. It happens that a small campfire is the smallest fire that is reliable and controllable. A still smaller flame is too easily snuffed out and a larger one too easily gets out of control. Prometheus was just large enough to feed the flames and to keep from getting burnt.

Similarly, points out Went, man was smart enough to develop speech, but first, in order to make sound, he had to be large enough to require lungs and to drive a forced stream of air.

In this review of the effects of size, we have touched

on Galileo's idea that the larger of two similar forms is the weaker. Let us conclude by giving Galileo's statement a little more attention.

Suppose, as shown in Figure 15, two apples are suspended, one with twice the diameter of the other. We know that the volume and the weight of the large apple is 2^3 or 8 times the volume and weight of the

15

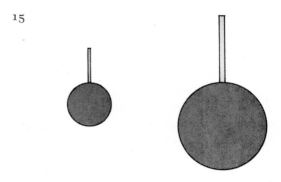

16

small one. If we also suppose the large stem to have twice the diameter of the small stem, we find that the strength of the stem, as given by the area of its cross section, is 2^2 or 4 times the strength of the small stem. Thus the weight of the apple — the load the stem must support — is eight times as much for the large apple as for the small, whereas the strength of the stem is only four times as much. Four times as much strength to resist eight times as much load: at some point, as the apple increases in size, it must fall from the tree.

Thus we are not surprised to see that the blossoms of the apple first stand erect on the branch; but as the apple develops, the stem is drawn to the side and down (Figure 16); and finally, when the apple is fully grown, the stem is pulled from the tree. We also observe that large fruits, like melons, squash, and pumpkins, do not hang from their stems at all but rest instead on the ground.

We can turn upside down our diagram of the apples hanging from stems and suppose them to sit on little pedestals. Our analysis of the strength of the pedestal

17

is essentially the same as for the stem, except that the pedestal is pushed down and put in compression rather than pulled down and put into tension. In both cases the cross-sectional area of the support goes up by a factor of four and the load to be supported by a factor of eight.

From considerations of how pedestals become relatively weaker as they and the bodies they support increase in size, we see why the trunk of a tree is proportionally thicker than the stem of a slender sapling, and the legs of an elephant are thicker and straighter too than those of a butterfly (Figure 17). We are assured, despite Gulliver's tale, that no giants have ever stalked the land. The sixty-foot Brobdingnagian that

Gulliver described would have weighed ninety tons — far too much for legs of flesh and bone. And even though steel and concrete are stronger than bone and living tissue, we observe that the Empire State Building is not as slender as a stalk of wheat — if it were, it would be only six feet wide at the base — another fact neatly observed by F. W. Went.

Another way in which a little pedestal may break is by bending or buckling. It can crimp and kick out to the side. In the analysis of bending in Figure 18, we see a beam that is pushed down in the center and up at the ends. The beam is bent so that the bottom is stretched, or put into tension, while at the same time the top is shortened, or put into compression. We might theorize therefrom that bending is the combination of tension and compression and that, as the beam increases in size, its resistance to bending grows more slowly than the force of the bending. Indeed, that is true, for, to put the matter precisely, a beam with twice the dimensions of another has only 2^3 or 8 times the section modulus or strength to overcome 2^4 or 16 times the bending moment introduced by its own weight. Thus any beam will break under its own weight if it is increased enough in size. So with regard to tension, compression, and bending too, Galileo was right: given an identity of shape and material, the larger of two forms is inevitably the weaker.

Galileo's observation has not been lost on today's engineers. When the behavior of a small model is used to simulate the behavior of a large structure, the most important consideration is to make the model weak enough, or, what amounts to the same thing, to make the loads on the model heavy enough. The engineer loads the structural members in the small model of the suspension bridge with sandbags to simulate the weight of those members when they are increased in size. Similarly, the engineer packs bags of mercury (which weighs nearly fourteen times as much as water), rather than water itself, against a small model of a dam in order to represent better the pressure of water against the real dam.

The two stratagems used by both nature and man to

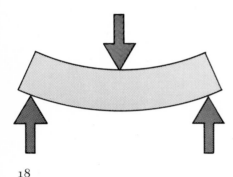

18

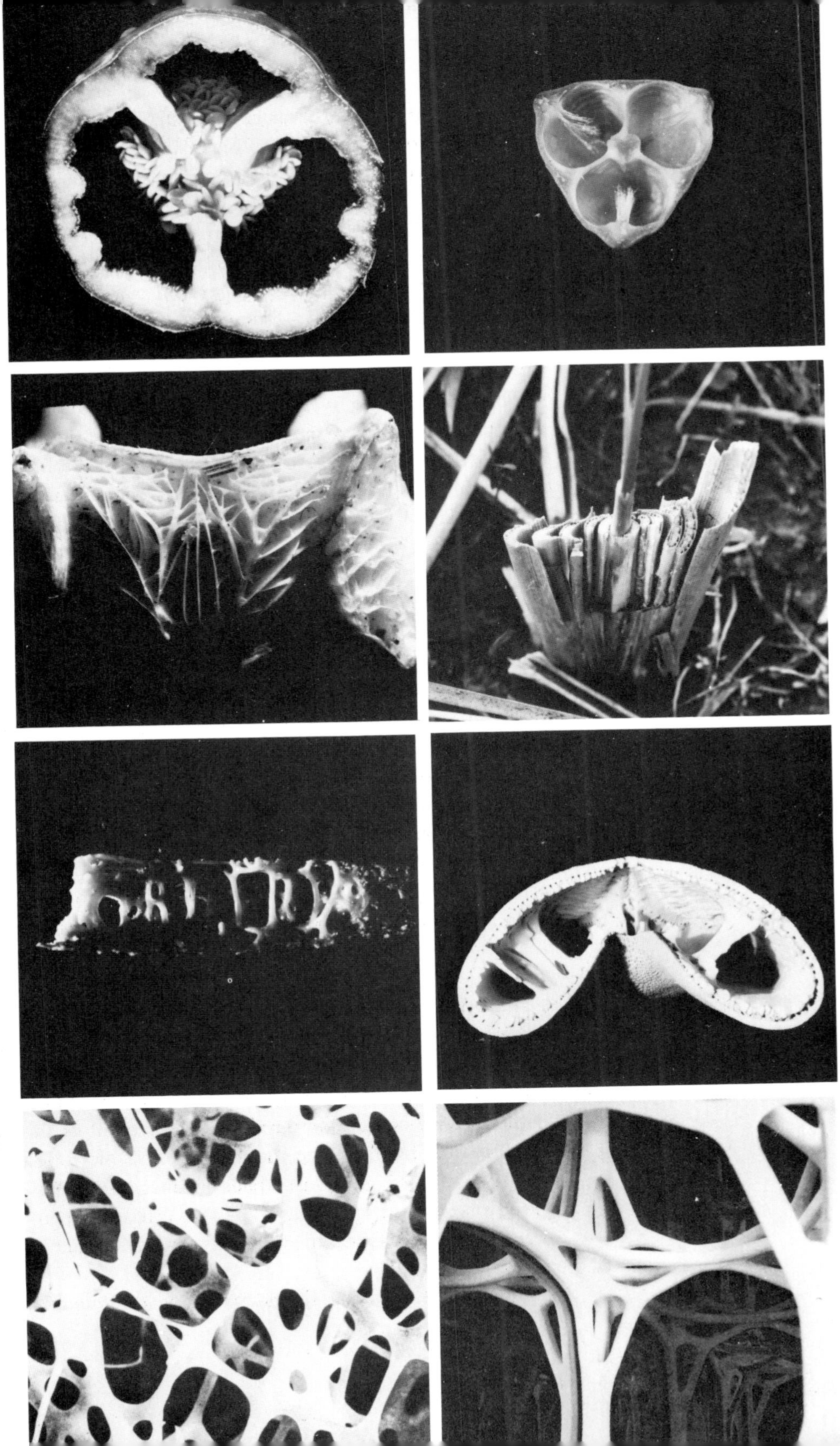

19*a* *b* *c* *d* *e* *f* *g* *h*

overcome the effects of increasing size are either to use a stronger material or to make the structure hollow and reduce its weight. Changing the material works only up to a point. Any material will eventually break under its own weight. A free-hanging chain of pure silica glass or steel, for example, can be longer than one of aluminum, and longer still can be a free-hanging length of boron — some 189.4 miles. But each material has its upper limit of size, and at some magnitude it will be unable to support itself.

The other way to overcome the effects of scale is to arrange material in a more effective configuration, to cut it away where it is not needed and to add it where it is required. That is perhaps the more frequent stratagem. It is the stratagem of design. We see in Figure 19 that with an interior cavity, an intact exterior, and a simple triangulation of ribs, the hollow pepper (a) and the seedpod (b) have less weight than they would if solid — but that they have an equivalent strength. The vertebra of the fish and the corrugated pith of the grass (c and d) also display hollowness, lightness, and ribbed strength. Between the top and bottom shells in both the horseshoe crab and the sea biscuit (e and f) the reinforcement is irregular, as if formed by the solidification of a sticky fluid. Frame g shows a magnified section of bone in the human tibia, photographed by Carl Struve, while h is a photograph of a structural study by Frei Otto in collaboration with Koch and Minke. Both are variations on the same theme — the reduction of mass in order to increase strength.

The ancient Romans used the same stratagem of design when they put light pumice aggregate and hollow earthenware pots in the concrete of the dome of the Pantheon. Their use of sunken panels or coffers on the interior of the dome reduced the weight of the structure still further. The modern-day use of ribbed construction, box sections, space frames, T beams, folded plates, and trusses are likewise attempts to reduce weight while leaving enough material intact to preserve strength.

Figure 20 shows the theme pavilions designed by

20a   b   c

d   e   f   g

Affleck, Desbarats, Dimakopoulos, Lebensold and Sise (top three photographs) and the United States Pavilion designed by Buckminster Fuller for Montreal's Expo '67 (next three photographs). Those structures are some of man's more recent attempts to build triangulated and open networks of steel. Their openness is a necessary concomitant of their size. Less material means less weight to support.

It is interesting to observe that like any of the regular or semiregular polyhedrons that contain pentagons, Fuller's dome, if made as a complete sphere, must contain twelve and only twelve pentagons. We see one of them in the center of frame e.

Also of interest is that the overall geometry of the dome is similar to the structure of certain microscopic viruses and radiolaria. Frame g shows some skeletal fragments of radiolaria magnified about one hundred times. Despite a sometimes similar geometry, the difference in absolute size between the radiolarian and the dome dictates important differences in their structure. Since the tubes at the bottom of the dome carry more load than the tubes at the top, they have greater wall thicknesses and greater strength. You cannot see that difference in tube thickness, since the outside diameters have been kept the same in order to facilitate the making of standard joints. But those differences exist, and, unlike the radiolarian — with its true spherical symmetry, able to spin, float, and bob in the waves unconcerned with which side is up or down, with such a small mass that it is uninfluenced by gravity — the dome is spherically symmetrical only in outward appearance; it cannot be flipped on its back like a radiolarian, but rather it is compelled to sit forever upright, with its weaker members at the top and its stronger members at the bottom, each specifically tailored to carry its assigned load.

The structural difference between the radiolarian and the dome is like that between the feather and the leaflets of the frond of the coconut palm (Figure 21.) Although both the feather and the frond have a central rib that gives rise to an even distribution of secondary filaments, the parts of the feather, being small, are relatively smooth and undifferentiated, whereas those of the frond are folded and more complex so as to support better their greater weight. The central mast of the frond is triangular and is joined in triangular intersections by folded leaflets which themselves are marked with central ribs.

One final example of the effect of scale in architecture is the plain but largely unnoticed fact that large buildings are taller and slenderer in their proportions than small buildings. The Empire State Building, although not as slender, comparatively speaking, as a reed, is still more slender than a one-story office building, and the apartment tower is still a tower rather than a cubical box like the single-family house. Ranko Bon, who has made statistical studies of building forms, points out that the differences in shape

21

between large buildings and small do not arise because of structural considerations but because rooms in houses and apartments are about the same size, and in both building types it is desirable to have as many rooms as possible exposed to the exterior. Thus, when the large building with its greater number of rooms increases its critical surface — its exterior — it elongates its form. Just as with a living organism then, its absolute size determines its shape.

2

Basic Patterns

So then always that knowledge is worthiest . . .
which considereth the simple forms or differences
of things, which are few in number, and the degrees
and coordinations whereof make all this variety.

— FRANCIS BACON

Basic Patterns

WE HAVE SEEN that space permits the existence of only a few regular polyhedrons and mosaics. In this chapter we will examine some less regular patterns. The chapter is short, the figures being the most important part, but it provides the key to all that follows, for by examining the geometric properties of quasi-regular patterns we can gain some insight into why nature prefers one over another. We can learn why spirals, meanders, and certain arrangements of branching patterns are so prevalent and why one thing looks so often like something else that is fundamentally different.

With regard to how patterns and shapes come into being, we can readily accept the fundamental idea of the theory of evolution, that things evolve to their fittest form; we can accept the principle that things tend toward a configuration with the least energy, that is to say, with the tightest fit, the lowest altitude, or the least motion; we can even accept the theory that the existing forms of nature are exactly those that are most likely to exist — taking into account all possible possibilities. But what forms, we wonder, are the fittest, the least energetic, and the most probable? Can we spell them out in advance? Can we define them other than by asserting redundantly that they are the end products of the struggle to survive, the dissipation of energy, and blind luck? By just looking at the geometrical properties of the possible distributions of material in space, can we predict what distributions will be favored in what context?

Perhaps we can. In plane geometry, for instance, we learn that a straight line is the direct path between two fixed points, and that the line of a circle is a collection of points equidistant from one fixed point. In nature we see the combination of the straight path and the circle when water flows more-or-less straight in a stream and then comes to rest in a more or less circular pond. Knowing both the properties of water and the properties of lines and circles, we can predict that water will flow and come to rest in those particular geometric shapes. We can predict a priori the outlines of streams and ponds, just as, once again on the basis of the geometry of lines and circles, we can predict that celestial bodies travel straight in empty space and in circular or elliptical orbits when captured by the gravitational fields of still larger bodies.

We might note in passing that the lines and circles adopted by natural forms are never perfect. Neither the stream nor the meteor runs perfectly straight, nor is the pond or orbital trajectory a perfect circle. Straight lines and circles are only the pure forms. They occur under only the simplest conditions. In nature, however, conditions are never entirely simple, and any "elementary" or "isolated" part is embedded in a larger system that operates in turn within other still larger systems. To some extent, then, the part is acted upon by the whole — by the totality of all the systems — and it never exactly fits an easily definable pattern. The warning is clear: nature never conforms precisely to our simple models; she introduces modifications as dictated by her lawful response to a multiplicity of demands.

Knowing that we deal only with oversimplified cases, let us continue. Let us generate some simple patterns by means of a straightforward exercise. Let us connect the dots in the array shown in Figure 22 so that all the dots link up with the center dot, either directly or indirectly, but so that any two dots connect along only one path. In that exercise we can think of the center dot as a center of growth, and that the growth radiates outward directly or indirectly so as

22

to reach each one of the outlying dots. It turns out that we can draw a number of different patterns that meet those requirements and that the different patterns have different geometrical attributes.

First, with regard to the array of points, we observe that every point is surrounded by six others in a regular manner, so as to maintain the same distance between nearest neighbors. It is at least of passing interest to learn that such an arrangement of points is possible only in a plane. If a constant distance is maintained between adjacent points on a sphere, for instance, every point can be surrounded by three, four, or five points — but not six. That analysis takes us back to considerations of regular forms, and a quick check reveals indeed that each of the regular polyhedrons of Figure 5 has its points or corners arranged on the surface of an imaginary sphere so that every corner is surrounded identically by three, four, or five others.

Attending to our regular arrangement of points, we find it an easy matter, as shown in Figure 23a, to start in the center of the array and spiral outward so as to sweep up all the points. Alternatively, as shown in frame b, we can start in the center and jog this way and that so as to join the dots with a long meandering line. The spiral and meander have exactly the same length. If we set the distance between adjacent dots equal to one unit, they both have a length of 90 units. Furthermore, if, in counting distances, we consider the path from the center point to the first point, the path from the center point through the first point to the second point, and the path from the center point through the first and second points to the third point, etc., as separate paths, then the average of all such paths, in both the meander and the spiral, is 45.5 units. We will find that number useful when we compare other patterns.

Figure 24 shows an entirely different way to connect the dots. The center is connected directly to each of the outlying dots in the pattern of an explosion. The total of all the separate radiating lines turns out to be 233.1 units, considerably more than the 90 units of the

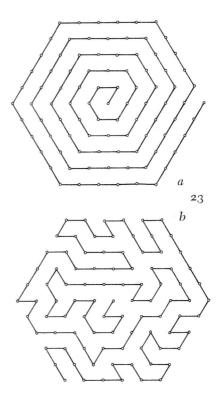

23

a

b

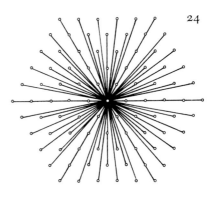

24

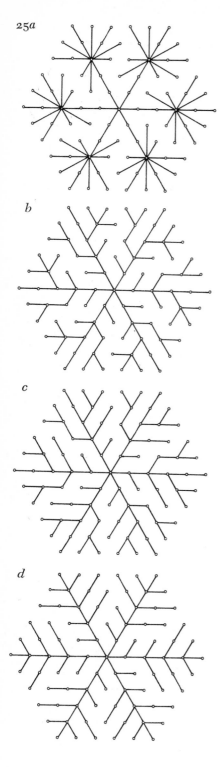

25a

b

c

d

spiral and the meander; and the average path, computed as before by finding the mean of the distances from all outlying points to the center, turns out to be only 3.37 units, considerably less than 45.5 units for the spiral and meander. The explosion thus has a much larger total length of path but a much shorter average length than the first two patterns. It uses a greater length of line to connect the dots, but it makes the connections more directly. Now consider branching patterns. Once again, in Figure 25a, the center point connects with all the other points, but each of the six arms of the figure terminates in a cluster of simple branches. The total length of path is 107.6 units, less than half the total length in the explosion. The average length is 4.25 units.

Figure 25b shows a pattern in which the secondary as well as the main branches have branched. The total length of path is only 90 units, the same as for the spiral, and the average path is only 3.73 units, not much more than the 3.37 of the explosion. A still shorter length of average path is found in the branching patterns of frames c and d. There the total length of path is again 90 units, but the average length is only 3.67 units.

What do those patterns tell us? They reveal, among other things, that spirals and explosions represent two extremes. The spiral is short, but it connects the points in an extremely circuitous manner. It might be a good path for a foraging worm or a visitor at a museum. It is interesting that both Frank Lloyd Wright and Le Corbusier designed spiral museums. Wright's was a circular spiral, the Solomon R. Guggenheim Museum in New York City, and Le Corbusier's a square spiral, the "Museum of Unlimited Expansion," a prototypical model that had several variants. Clearly, however, a spiral is not at all a suitable form for a tree which must transport nutrients between its central trunk and outermost leaves along a reasonably direct path. The pattern of the explosion, on the other hand, minimizes travel distance between the center and each outlying point, but the total of all the travel distances is enormous. The pattern of the explosion might be suitable for flinging rocks across the landscape, but it is not suitable for a tree: a tree cannot sustain each of its leaves with a separate branch.

It turns out that branching patterns are compromises between the single circuitous route of the spiral and the many direct routes of the explosion. Branching patterns obtain a short total length at the expense of only a little indirectness here and there. They effect a savings in the whole at the expense of only a few of the parts. Actually, they are incredibly good compromises. They may have no more total length than a spiral (in fact they may even be shorter than a spiral, as we shall see) and only a slightly longer average path than the minimum found in the explosion. Branching, therefore, commands the best of both worlds: shortness as well as directness.

Figure 26 shows a branching pattern that has less length of line than any of the other patterns. Its total length is 77.9 units, 13 percent less than the 90 units of the spiral and the meander. The pattern is characterized by joints in which lines meet three at a time at 120 degrees to one another. We will study the pattern in more detail later, but here let us observe that with its minimum *overall* length it represents one pole or extreme of branching, the other pole being the explosion pattern with a minimum *average* length. Note that the branching pattern with three-way joints has an average path of 4.2 units — more than the explosion or some of the other branching patterns.

Already, then, we have discovered several prototypical patterns: the spiral, the meander, the explosion, and various forms of branching. We can describe those patterns explicitly in terms of four geometric attributes: 1, uniformity; 2, space filling; 3, overall length; and 4, directness.

The spiral is beautifully uniform; it curves around on itself in a perfectly regular manner. It can fill all of two-dimensional space, being capable of infinite expansion, and it is also quite short. But as we have seen, as measured by the mean of distances to its center, the spiral is extremely indirect.

The random meander turns out to be much like the

26

27a

b

spiral except that it is not uniform; it is quite turbulent and chaotic. Nevertheless, like the spiral, it can cover all of two-dimensional space, it is short, and it is indirect.

The explosion is uniform in that it maintains constant angles between its rays. Note, however, that unlike the spiral or meander, it cannot fill all of space uniformly: it is much more dense close to the source than far away. Furthermore, as we have seen, the sum of its constituent rays becomes very large. Nevertheless, it excels in directness — linking each point to the center as directly as possible.

Branching patterns are less uniform and display more variations in their details than either spirals or explosions, but they fill all of space, they are short, and they are relatively direct. In addition, the branching pattern with regular triple junctions is shorter than any of the other patterns.

We have not examined natural occurrences of those patterns, but on the basis of their geometrical attributes alone we can see why they might be adopted by natural forms. Different arrangements have different spatial advantages. Thus, in the distribution of blood vessels, the route of a subway system, or the design of forked columns to carry a roof where both overall length and directness are important, the same branching pattern might turn out to be advantageous. We see that certain patterns bring certain benefits and efficiencies, irrespective of the size of the system, the forces, or the particular materials used.

By way of example, Figure 27 shows architectural models of branched columns. The columns in Antoni Gaudi's model of the *Sagrada Familia* (a), like those in Frei Otto's structural study (b), support the roof at many points, enabling it to be thin and light. The branching of each column joins the points of the roof to a single point on the floor with a small amount of material laid out in a reasonably direct route. If the branches of each column traveled directly from each point of the roof to a single point on the floor, or if each point of the roof was supported by a separate column, more material would be used, and since the separate branches or columns would be longer, they would be more likely to buckle and bend.

At this point we should note that still other geometric attributes could be used to describe our patterns. We could, for example, work with the total of all the separate paths before we take their average; and we could consider average distances from every point, as well as from the center. By examining those or still other attributes, we might establish a different grouping or hierarchy of patterns. And just as our present grouping leads to valid conclusions about why nature adopts a specific pattern in a specific instance, other hierarchies based on other geometrical attributes would be similarly revealing.

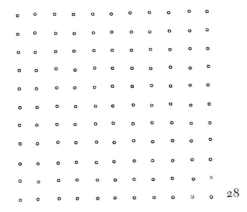

28

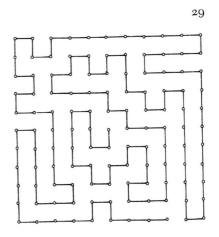

29

Our patterns, even if they are not the only possible distinctly different ones, arise quite naturally, as we have seen, from interconnections among points arranged in a triangular array. They also arise from interconnections of points in a square array like that shown in Figure 28. We can easily make a random meander, as depicted in Figure 29. If the distance between points that are nearest neighbors is set equal to one unit, the total length of line is 120 units. The distance along the line from each point to the center turns out to be, for the average case, 60.5 units.

The simple spiral and its numerous variations are

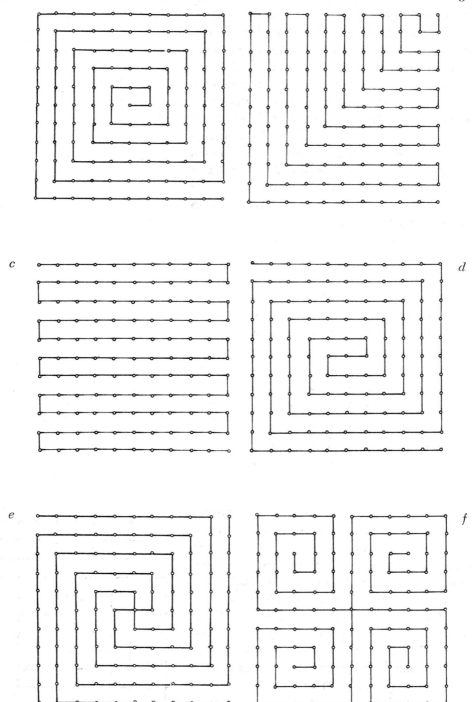

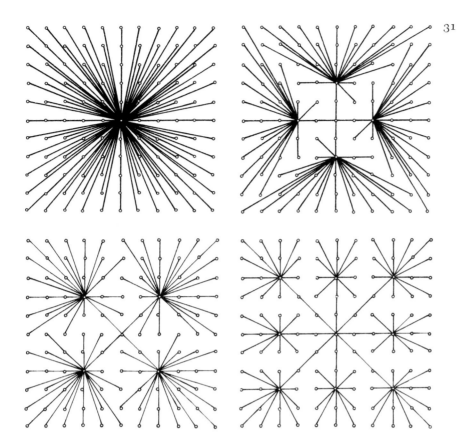

also obtainable, as depicted in Figure 30. All the examples have a total length of 120 units. The simplest spiral (*a*) has an average distance from each point to the center point of 60.5 units. Meander (*b*) has an average path of 37.7 units. Both meander (*c*) and the double spiral (*d*) have an average path of 30.5 units, and both quadruple spirals (*e* and *f*) have average paths of 15.5 units. Thus, branching at the center reduces the average distance — that is to say, connects the outlying points more directly.

Explosion patterns are shown in Figure 31. The lengths of lines in the four frames are 364.8, 280.2, 228.4, and 160.0. The more the explosion branches, the less total length of line it uses. Note, however, that none of the branched forms has as low an average path

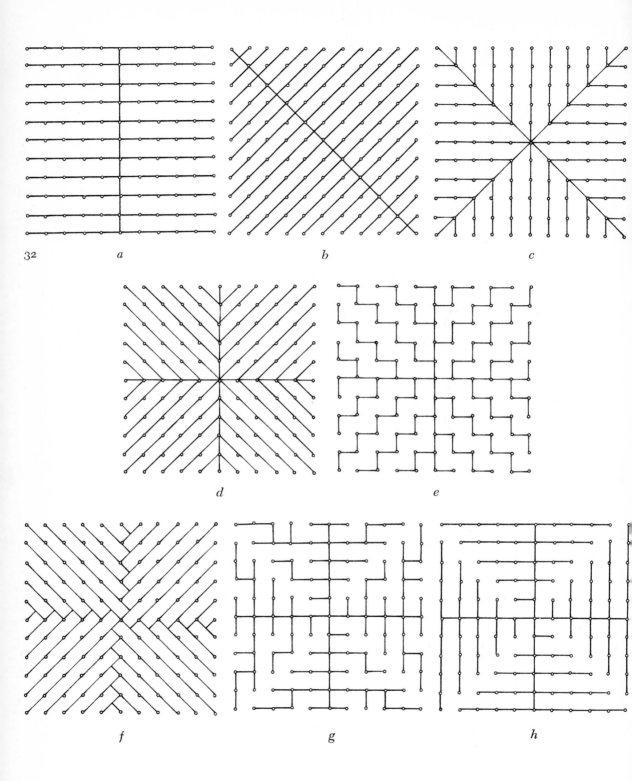

32   *a*   *b*   *c*

d   *e*

f   *g*   *h*

as the simple form. The numerical values for average path in the four frames are 4.0, 4.7, 5.0, and 4.8 units.

Figure 32 shows various other branching patterns. Most of them are both short and direct. Frames *a* and *b* with central stems have total lengths of 120 and 155.1 units, and average paths of 5.5 and 5.2 units. Frames *c* and *d* with four-way stems have total lengths of 128.3 and 161.4 units, and an average length of 4.4 units. The right-angled jogging pattern and the basket-weave pattern have total lengths of 120 and 155.1, and averages of 5.5 and 4.5. The patterns in the last two frames each have a total length of 120 units and an average length of 5.5 units.

The shortest branched network is again the pattern with three-way joints, depicted in Figure 33. It interconnects the points with a path 109.5 units long, as against 120 units for the simple spiral. The configuration is quite indirect, however; it has an average path of 9.3 units, compared with 4 units in the explosion.

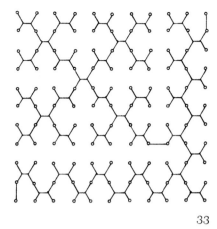

33

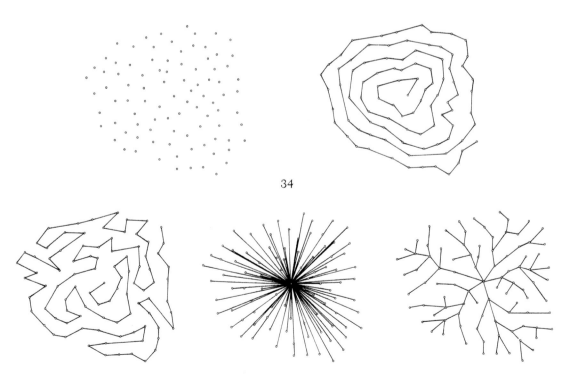

34

Furthermore, we find the same patterns within an array of randomly distributed points. Figure 34 shows again examples of spiral, meandering, explosive, and branching patterns. In each configuration, every point connects with the center point along a unique route. The configurations are more haphazard and capricious than those that arise from regular arrays of points, but each of them represents just as clearly a distinctly different pattern.

In three dimensions, the same patterns also arise. The spiral becomes a corkscrew or helix (which does not fill all of space like its two-dimensional analogue), the random meander becomes an intricate three-dimensional snarl, like a tangle of string, and the explosion and branching patterns take on three-dimensional forms that are immediately analogous to their two-dimensional counterparts.

Topology

BEFORE EXPLORING EXAMPLES of those designs as found in nature, let us review one last aspect of patterns, an aspect that shows dramatically how their attributes are decided by the constraints of space. In each of the patterns, the relation between the number of lines and the number of points is precisely the same: the lines always number one less than the points. That restrictive relation holds for every pattern that does not contain loops, that has only one line between any two points. In an example of a single line which connects but two points, we can readily see that the number of lines stands at one less than the number of points. For the simplest spiral of Figure 30 we can also see that the relation holds, but for the complicated branching pattern of Figure 33 the constancy of the relation is no longer obvious. Still, every one of our patterns obeys the rule.

The interesting idea here is that in any given pattern the points that unite many lines balance the points that join only one. That balance or trade-off enables the overall number of points and lines to differ by exactly one. The trade-off occurs automatically, of course, with no thought on the part of the pattern or the pencil that draws the pattern. It is determined by space itself. We can describe the trade-off in terms of a simple topological equation. If, in accord with Figure 35, we call the number of one-way joints (points at the ends of lines) J_1, the number of two-way joints (points that join two lines) J_2, the number of three-way joints (points that join three lines) J_3, etc., we can write the formula

$$1 \, J_1 \pm 0 \, J_2 - 1 \, J_3 - 2 \, J_4 - \ldots = 2$$

The simple spiral of Figure 30a has two one-way joints that mark its beginning and end, plus 119 two-way joints. In terms of the formula, then,

$$1 \, (2) \pm 0 \, (119) = 2$$

The simple explosion of Figure 31a has 80 one-way joints, 40 two-way joints, and 1 eighty-way joint, so that

$$1 \, (80) \pm 0 \, (40) - 78 \, (1) = 2$$

Similarly, the second branching pattern in Figure 31b with 80 one-way joints, 36 two-way joints, 1 four-way joint, and 4 twenty-one way joints has a formula of

$$1 \, (80) \pm 0 \, (36) - 2 \, (1) - 19 \, (4) = 2$$

Every pattern comes out right. Every pattern without loops that we or nature can make obeys the same mathematical expression.

We might observe that looped patterns with more than one route between points, that is to say, patterns with enclosed areas, such as the one shown in Figure 36, also obey strict mathematical laws. Those patterns fall into only seventeen distinct symmetry groups. Every two-dimensional repetitive figure, be it in brickwork, textiles, wallpaper, modules of city planning, or in the arrangement of molecules in the cross section of a crystal, is but a variation on one of those seventeen groups. The groups are made by the regular translation, rotation, and reflection of their parts. They are

J_1

J_2

J_3

J_4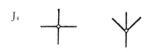

J_6

35

36

beyond the scope of this study, but their finite number illustrates once again how limited are the possibilities of spatial arrangement.

3

All Things Flow

Can anyone understand the spreading of the clouds . . . ?

— Job 36:29

ACCORDING to the ancient philosopher Heraclitus, the sole actuality of nature resides in change. All things are becoming. All things are flowing. At the same time, however, all things remain the same. The modern physicist wrestles with that paradox when he studies flow and turbulence. The new water chases out the old, but the pattern remains the same.

Turbulence

TURBULENCE forms the primordial pattern, the chaos that was "in the beginning." We are all familiar with turbulence. We have poured cream into coffee and watched the white marbled swirls as they curl and twist. We have watched the smoke from the fire stream upward and break into whirls and eddies. But the exact visual pattern is difficult to describe. Turbulence does not fit precisely any of the simple patterns that we generated in the last chapter. To some extent turbulence resembles the random meanders of Figures 23*b* and 29, and it happens that any particular particle within a turbulent flow does indeed describe an erratic and meandering path. But turbulent flows also have eddies and whirls like the configurations of Figures 23*a* and 30*a*. In fact, it is the eddies that distinguish turbulent from nonturbulent or laminar flow.

We will study spiral patterns more fully in the next chapter, but here let us observe that the spiral eddy comes into existence when a stream gets stalled against its boundaries or against another stream moving in the opposite direction. The stalled stream breaks into pieces that roll over on themselves. Right at the boundary, the flow of the stream has zero velocity — which is why little particles of dust can ride on the blade of a fan without being blown off, and why you cannot blow fine pieces of dust from the surface of a table — only large pieces that stick up into the breeze. At increasing distances from the boundary, the flow moves with higher velocities, and the difference in rates of flow causes the stream to trip over itself, to curl around on itself, just as a wave curls when it stubs its toe rushing up the beach.

Although we expect to find eddies in turbulent flow, we do not know when any specific eddy will come into being or die away. We cannot yet predict how eddies interact. Similarly, we know as a general rule that any particle within a turbulent flow gets knocked about in an aimless fashion by the swirls, so that it describes an erratic meandering path, but at any given moment we cannot predict the precise location or velocity of the particle. Our inability to predict details of turbulent flow hampers us in many fields. We find it difficult to forecast the weather, interpret sunspots, ascertain the flow of material beneath the earth's crust, or even to predict the exact pressure required to force a large volume of water through a long pipe. Much about turbulence, like the spreading of the clouds, remains beyond our understanding.

But even if we cannot predict all the details, we can predict something about the average case. We can consider the unpredictable local velocities and pressures as chance or random occurrences and then, with the aid of probability theory, take the mean of those occurrences and obtain mathematical descriptions of average motions in average flows.

Just because such an analysis treats the eddies as random occurrences, we should not be misled into believing that they really are random. An eddy is determined by other eddies, and those in turn are determined by still others, and so forth, back to certain specific initial conditions. But we cannot yet describe the initial conditions with enough accuracy to be able to predict all the resulting consequences. The initial conditions contain so many factors that compete with and countermand one another that we are forced to treat the resulting eddies as chance events. When we do, we get results that describe the average, that is to say, the most probable case.

The analysis of turbulence in terms of probability reveals several interesting things about eddies. For instance, the average eddy moves a distance about equal to its own diameter before it generates small eddies that move, more often than not, in the opposite direction. Those smaller eddies generate still smaller eddies and the process continues until all the energy dissipates as heat through molecular motion. In 1941, A. N. Kolmogoroff first set forth the idea that turbulence generates a hierarchy of eddies, thereby inspiring the beautifully apt verse of L. F. Richardson:

> Big whirls have little whirls,
> That feed on their velocity;
> And little whirls have lesser whirls,
> And so on to viscosity.

Through statistical analysis, Kolmogoroff also predicted that the velocity of an eddy is proportional to the cube root of its size, that, for example, an eddy moving twice as fast as another will usually be eight times as large, or that one moving ten times as fast will be a thousand times as large.

Reynolds Number

STILL ANOTHER WORK of a theoretical and statistical nature, this time by Werner Heisenberg, shows why density, viscosity, and the width of a stream all play a part in the visual appearance of turbulence — just as Osborne Reynolds observed (without being able to explain) about ninety years ago. Reynolds's discovery, as expressed by the concept of the Reynolds number, shows how things can change their shape in response to a change in scale, and yet, at the same time, and in seeming contradiction, have the same shape at different scales. Let us examine that idea.

We can arrive at the concept of the Reynolds number by asking four simple questions: 1, Does turbulence increase or decrease with an increase in the velocity of the stream? 2, Does turbulence increase or decrease with an increase in the size of an obstacle in the stream? 3, Does turbulence increase or decrease with an increase in the density of material that makes up the stream? 4, Does turbulence increase or decrease with an increase in the viscosity of the material of the stream?

The answers, for the most part, are easy. 1, Turbulence increases as the velocity increases. The flag flutters more in the gale than in the zephyr. 2, Turbulence increases as the size of the obstacle increases. The freighter creates more wake than the dinghy. 3, Turbulence increases as the density of the material increases. With greater density, more particles are present to get jostled about: more interaction can, and therefore will, take place. 4, Turbulence decreases with an increase in viscosity. Here we need to know that viscosity is a measure of the internal friction of the stream, the ability of the stream to stick together, to withstand shear. Realizing that air or water with low viscosity is easily made turbulent when it flows around an obstacle, while oil or molasses with high viscosity oozes smoothly around an obstacle without eddies and backwash, we conclude that turbulence is inversely proportional to viscosity: the greater the viscosity the less the turbulence.

We can write the answers to the four questions in mathematical shorthand by saying that turbulence, T, is directly proportional to velocity, obstacle size, and density — V, S, and D — but it is inversely proportional to viscosity, v. Mathematically then:

$$T \propto V$$

$$T \propto S$$

$$T \propto D$$

$$D \propto \frac{1}{v}$$

or, putting all the terms together,

$$T \propto \frac{V \cdot S \cdot D}{v}$$

We can also go a bit further, just as Reynolds did, for, if we choose our dimensional units in the right way, we can get them to cancel so that T becomes a dimensionless number, the so-called Reynolds number R, and we have

$$R = \frac{V \cdot S \cdot D}{v}$$

Now, the beauty of that derivation lies in the fact that flows with the same Reynolds number look much the same, whereas flows with different Reynolds numbers look quite different. We can combine different velocities, obstacle sizes, densities, and viscosities in different ways, but if we get the same Reynolds number, we will get the same general appearance. Thus, for example, whether a fast-flowing stream is obstructed by a pebble or a slow-moving stream by a boulder, the same pattern of backwash is produced. A speck of dust falls through the air with as much difficulty as our bodies might experience in moving through molasses. Those cases of dynamic similarity are of great interest to the engineer who sets up tests of small models in order to predict the behavior of full-scale structures. The engineer plays the variables of velocity, size, density, and viscosity against one another in any number of ways, but if the variables balance out to the same result, to the same Reynolds number, to the same amount of turbulence, then the flows look roughly equivalent.

Concentrating on obstacles for a moment, we can see that a change in size results in a change in pattern or form. The small object disturbs the stream but little, the large object creates a turbulent wake. Instead of considering the size of an obstruction, we can also consider the size of a pipe through which the stream might flow. Whereas the large rock directly disrupts the flow, the large pipe allows the flow to disrupt itself. The large pipe has more room for turbulence and thus more turbulence arises. In fact, we can generate Reynolds numbers based on diameters of pipes exactly as we can for numbers based on diameters of obstructions. In both cases the pattern of flow changes with size.

Remembering, however, that decreasing the velocity or density, or increasing the viscosity, can compensate for the effect of increasing size, we see why flows of different sizes can look much the same. Changing only one variable definitely alters the appearance, but changing two or more together may well leave the appearance unaffected. The principle of compensation among variables explains why we find similar patterns at vastly different scales.

One further point should be made about scale and turbulence. Turbulence, or its measure — Reynolds number — is itself an expression of quantity or size. The Reynolds number is a measure of the *amount* of material that is present. Considering flow in a pipe, we can see that increasing the velocity of the flow, the size of the pipe, or the density of the material are simply three different ways to get a greater quantity of material to interact with itself.

The Turbulence of the Universe

It is no coincidence that milk poured into a wet sink imitates the design of galaxies and clusters of galaxies in the sky (Figure 37). Differences in velocities, densities, and viscosities compensate for the enormous difference in size between the kitchen sink

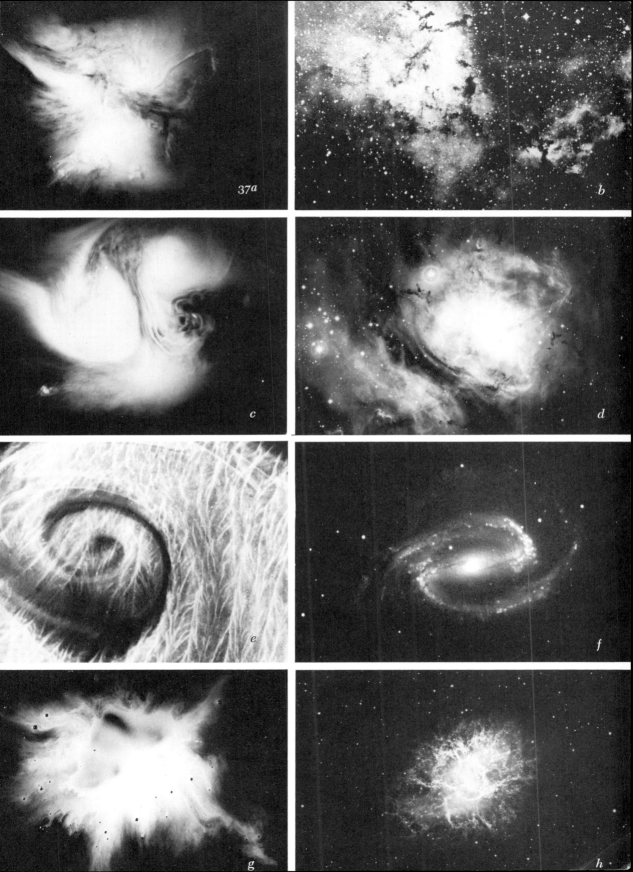

37a
b
c
d
e
f
g
h

and the heavens, so that the milk and the Milky Way follow a similar plan.

By way of illustration, Figure 37 shows four pairs of pictures. With the exception of *e,* in which the swirling material is a mixture of glycerin, food coloring, and ink, the first frame of each pair shows milk that has been spilled in a black slate sink. The milk covers areas a few inches across, while the gas clouds, spiral galaxies, and exploding Crab Nebula with which the milk is compared cover areas in the order of ten quintillion (10^{19}) miles across.

Kant and Laplace first described the turbulence of stellar material; Van Gogh's painting, *Starry Night,* gave it visual expression (Figure 38); and Carl von Weizsäcker and George Gamow have attempted to explain the physical facts.

At an early stage, the material of the universe was a gas of nuclear particles. The gas was necessarily turbulent, that is to say, its Reynolds number was necessarily high, because the "pipe" in which it flowed, the absolute size of the universe, was large and did not restrict its flow. The turbulence of the gas gave rise to local compressions and rarefactions. Once the particles of gas were compressed, the gravitational attraction between them increased — their attraction for one another being inversely related as d^2, the square of their separation. It happened that many of the compressed clumps could not expand again: they were held in check by their own gravity. It is interesting to know that similar clumpings of gas take place in the turbulent air around us every day, but that those clumps are too small to hold together under the influence of their own gravitational pull. The clumps of primordial gas, however, were enormously larger. They had a mass several million times the mass of the sun. In such a large clump, the increased gravitational attraction pulled the particles still closer together, increasing the strength of the attraction still more, which in turn pulled the particles closer again. Thus, once a large enough clump had formed, it collapsed on itself in an ever-accelerating gravitational rush.

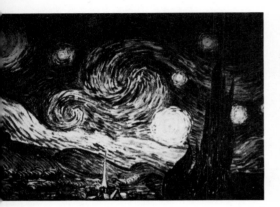

38

If the clump of gas was very large, the collapse might continue indefinitely — down to almost nothing. At this very moment there may be billions of such collapsing clumps in the sky. They are the "black holes" that astronomers are looking for, so designated because their immense gravitational attraction makes it impossible for any material to get out, not even particles of light. Of course, they are not really holes. Just the opposite: they are immense concentrations of material that suck everything around them, including light itself, into their interiors. Since no light escapes, we have no way of seeing them directly. Consequently, they have the appearance of black emptinesses.

What happens in the hole, and how matter escapes from becoming infinitely collapsed, remains one of the most pressing questions in physics. What happens in the hole may foretell what will happen to the entire universe, when and if it collapses on itself prior to its next round of expansion. Somehow, according to John Wheeler, material in the hole has the opportunity to take on new spatial properties. Somehow, a new cycle with a new spatial topology starts over again.

When the clumps of primordial nuclear gas are small, the contraction is stopped by centrifugal force before the stage of the black hole is reached. The random motions within the small clump inevitably cause it to rotate, to behave like an eddy, and the more it shrinks, the faster it spins, like a whirling skater when he pulls in his arms. That increase in rotation leads to an increase in centrifugal force that tends to throw material outward, and soon, in the plane of rotation, material gets flung away from the center in long spiral arms. Perpendicular to the plane of rotation, however, material still moves inward, collapse still goes on, and the whole system flattens into the familiar disk of a spiral galaxy.

The mechanism that keeps the spiral arms of the galaxy spread out, that prevents them from wrapping up, is still not completely understood. As an analogy though, you might consider a rotating water sprinkler that throws out spiral arms of water. Like that sprin-

39

kler, a galaxy flings out arms, and the material in the arms feeds into the system from above and below the rotating disk.

Figure 39 shows another analogue of the spiral galaxy, an old millstone that has been cut with spiral tracks that carry ground grain outward from the center as the stone revolves.

When clumps of gas rotate slowly, they do not fling themselves out into spiral arms; they remain smooth and their collapse results in elliptical galaxies.

A similar theory of turbulence and rotation accounts for the formation of the solar system. Laplace assumed that the sun and planets condensed out of a great revolving gaseous cloud. Today we postulate that collections of dust as well as condensations of gas are at work. The particles of dust, incidentally, may have been driven together initially by the pressure of starlight — a force that once again varies inversely with d^2, the square of the separation between particles. According to modern theory, flows of gas and dust break up into turbulent eddies. Those eddies conflict with one another and kill each other off, except for the ones that stay clear of collisions. It happens, not unexpectedly, that the eddies that remain, those that avoid collisions, are spaced at regular intervals from one another. Those eddies condense further and give birth to planets, so that the planets too end up with a regular spacing. The particulars of the theory thus explain why each successive planet in the solar system is about twice as far from the sun as the previous one.

In that story of the creation of the planets we see a kind of evolutionary theory at work. We see the decimation of the unfit, the swirls that collide with one another, and the survival of the fit, the swirls that were originally positioned so as to avoid collision. The end result is an orderly arrangement that appears more a product of design than chance. Order is born out of chaos. It is interesting, however, that the chaos persists. In fact, considering the dissipated heat generated by the collisions of the eddies, and by the condensation of the dust and gas in forming the planets, the disorder or entropy of the system has actually increased. The order of the local events — the spacing of the planets — is more than recompensed by the disorder — the heat gain — in the rest of the universe.

Vortex Streets

WHEN WE CONSIDER flows with low Reynolds numbers, we see the production of large-scale order even more directly. At low Reynolds numbers, the eddies alternate with one another and form regular rows. Such flows are not really turbulent, nor are they steady; instead, they are "nearly steady" or periodic.

40

Behind a rock in a stream or a moving canoe paddle, you often see two oppositely swirling eddies. Behind a larger obstruction such as a bridge abutment in a fast-flowing river, you see those two eddies rhythmically peel off and flow downstream, first from one edge and then from the other. Figure 40 shows such an alternating stream of vortexes in a flow of air that has been filled with oil droplets from an aerosol spray. The air flows around a stationary cable to produce the periodic pattern called a vortex street. The vortex from one side of the cable grows until it draws material across its wake from the opposite side of the cable. That flow of material from the opposite side, which twists in the opposite direction, grows until it in turn draws material from the opposite side. The growth takes place periodically, first on one side of the cable and then on the other. Note that the eddies in the bottom row curl counterclockwise, whereas those in the top row curl clockwise. Where they intermingle in the center, the eddies interlock like rotating gears in a machine.

It has been suggested that swimming fish, which generate their own eddies, might take advantage of the rotations of those eddies and ride the meandering path between them like a moving belt riding between rollers (Figure 41a). Recently, however, Heinrich Hertel has determined, at least for a swimming snake, that the two rows of vortexes are squeezed into a single line and that the body of the animal cuts through the center of each vortex rather than wrapping around it (Figure 41 b). The interesting point is that no new eddies form behind the snake, that is to say, there is no backwash. Also, the eddies stay in position right where they are formed; they do not travel downstream. That lack of wake and eddy movement testifies to the efficiency of the snake's swimming motion.

It has also been hypothesized that birds travel in a vee formation in order to take advantage of each other's eddies and wakes. The reaction of each bird pushing down on the air below it creates an updraft around it. If other birds crowd in close, they can use those updrafts to keep themselves aloft. If the whole group flies in a vee, all the birds share approximately the same amount of updraft — since each bird flies forward into the updraft of the bird in front. The lead bird enjoys a boost too, since it is aided on both sides by the birds behind. Each individual bird thus rides the wake of its neighbors, and calculations reveal that a group of twenty-five birds can fly in formation some 70 percent farther than one bird alone.

41a

b

Human beings, as well as birds and snakes, make use of periodic patterns of flow — but in a rather unexpected way. We listen to them. If the vortexes in a vortex street peel away from the obstruction with a frequency between 50 and 20,000 hertz, or cycles per second, we hear melodious hums and whistles. Aeolian harps, tree limbs, telephone wires, flutes, organ pipes, and teakettles all produce sound by shedding vortexes within the audible range of frequencies.

We are occasionally affected by vortex streets at a much larger scale. We now know that regular vortexes caused the collapse of the Tacoma Narrows suspension bridge in 1940. With a steady wind of forty-two miles per hour blowing across a thirty-nine foot wide roadway, vortexes peeled off from one edge and then from the other and caused the bridge to twist on itself, first one way and then the other. After its collapse, the bridge was rebuilt with a box cross section rather than an H cross section so that it would better resist torsion or twisting, and all the surfaces of the box were made of open trusses in order to reduce the amount of material exposed to the wind — to reduce the area term in Reynolds's equation.

Stress and Flow

AT A STILL LOWER Reynolds number, flow does not produce eddies at all; it oozes smoothly around any obstacle in its path. Figure 42 shows the pattern of low-speed flow around a cylinder.

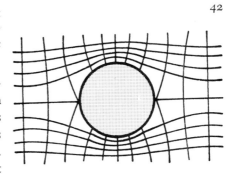

42

Figure 42 is a remarkable picture. It actually represents three entirely different physical phenomena. In addition to low-speed flow around a cylinder, it shows an electric dipole in a uniform electric field, and lines of tension and compression around a circular hole. Those three phenomena are basically different, but they have the same spatial configuration.

Interpreting the figure in terms of low-speed flow (or more correctly, irrotational flow, in which the fluid does not get stuck against the sides of the cylinder so as to produce eddies) the horizontal lines represent streamlines — paths of the water particles or paths of bits of dye that you might add to the water. Where the streamlines lie close together — above and below the cylinder in this particular figure — the velocity is high; and where they stand far apart — at the left and right in the figure — the velocity is low. The vertical lines at right angles to the streamlines are equipotentials. They are difficult to define in physical terms, but, analogous to electrical potentials, they are lines along which velocity potential does not change. In fluid flow, however, the important lines are the other ones, the streamlines.

One other fact about fluid flow that will help our understanding of the figure is that within a stream we can have a small source and a small sink — a place where additional fluid comes in and a place where it goes out — and if we move the source close to the sink, additional fluid will flow in and then out again without greatly disturbing the rest of the stream. If we choose the size of the source and the sink correctly, and set them the right distance apart, they will act exactly like a cylindrical obstruction in the stream. We can thus think of the shaded circle of our figure as containing a two-dimensional source and sink, around which flow the streamlines.

Now let us look at the figure entirely differently, as a picture of electrical forces. Instead of locating a source and a sink in a uniform flow, let us place a small positive and a small negative charge (called an electric dipole) in a uniform two-dimensional electric field. We then obtain exactly the same picture. The horizontal lines are lines of electrical force. The closer they are together the stronger is the electrical field. The vertical lines are again equipotentials. The amount of work that is performed in moving an electric charge in the field is measured by the number of equipotentials that the charge crosses.

Jumping once again to a different phenomenon, let us now suppose that you have a steel plate that is held at the ends and stretched. If the plate has a circular hole in it, the stress trajectories within the plate will look like the lines in the figure. Those lines that run from left to right will be lines of equal tension, and those that run up and down will be lines of equal compression. Where the lines are close together, the forces of tension or compression will be high; and where they are far apart, the forces will be low. If the plate fails, it will tear across the center of the hole just where the lines are tightly bunched.

So why does the same drawing depict those different phenomena?

Richard Feynman has supplied the answer. In discussing the "underlying unity" of nature, he cites the identity between the mathematical description of irrotational flow and the mathematical description of an electric dipole in a uniform field, and he also shows how those phenomena are mathematically equivalent to problems involving the flow of heat, stretched membranes, the diffusion of neutrons, and the uniform lighting of a plane. Then he says:

> The "underlying unity" might mean that everything is made out of the same stuff, and therefore obeys the same equations. That sounds like a good explanation, but let us think. The electrostatic potential, the diffusion of neutrons, heat flow — are we really dealing with the same stuff? Can we really imagine that the electrostatic potential is *physically* identical to the temperature, or to the density of particles? . . . The displacement of a membrane is certainly *not* like a temperature. Why, then, is there "an underlying unity"? . . .
>
> Is it possible that *this* is the clue? That the thing which is common to all the phenomena is the *space*, the framework into which the physics is put? As long as things are reasonably smooth in space, then the important things that will be involved will be the rates of change of quantities with position in space. That is why we always get an equation with a gradient. . . . What is common to all our problems is that they involve space. . . .

Returning then to our figure, we find that each

phenomenon for which it stands has some property that changes in magnitude, or in magnitude and direction, at different points in space. In the example of fluid flow, the streamlines change in magnitude and direction; in the example of the dipole in the electric field, the lines of force change in magnitude and direction; and in the case of the stretched plate, the trajectories of tension and compression change in magnitude. The lines of flow, force, or stress are not the same, but their changes are. Those changes take place in the same smooth and continuous manner.

Now consider how we show those smooth changes in our diagram. We divide the field or the space into separate pieces and draw lines that represent averages of the changes. It can be argued that by cutting up the field and taking averages we lose sight of the continuity of the phenomena — but we can make our slices as small as we want and the directness of our line drawing as a visual statement of change more than compensates for any losses introduced by subdividing the field.

The important point is that once we decide to represent a continuously changing gradient by means of "contour" lines, the question of how many different gradients can exist in space reduces to the question of how many different patterns of roughly parallel lines can we draw. The answer is, not many.

Our figure shows a pattern of more-or-less parallel lines that have been separated. It is the pattern you get if you stab a linen handkerchief with an icepick. The fibers separate and "flow" around the pick. (The analogy does not hold exactly, because the vertical lines — the warp, let us say — would not stay at right angles to the horizontal woof, as shown in the figure, unless the two were directly connected to one another.)

A simpler pattern of roughly parallel lines is the fan pattern in the straw fibers of a broom or, in the case of electrical phenomena, in the equipotentials at the ends of two parallel plates with opposite charge. Figure 43 is Clerk Maxwell's drawing of those equipotentials. The lines of force end at right angles to the plates and the equipotentials run lengthwise and parallel to the

43

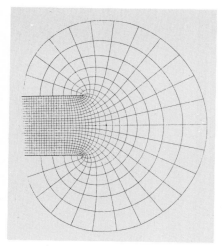

plates. Note how similar the pattern looks to a molasseslike flow issuing from a tube.

The spreading of lines may be less regular, of course, as in a lock or curl of hair. An interesting example is shown in Figure 44 in which the bud of a peony has been sliced to reveal the first stages in the development of its petals. How does the turbulent tissue sort itself into a symmetrical arrangement of petals? What breaks down the initially solid bud to start the process of differentiation? Stress? Electrical forces? Chemical action? It could be any of those, or something else. The pattern, however, is one of irregular streamlines.

We might note that Maxwell's drawing of lines of force in Figure 43 is a little misleading since it shows the equipotentials ending on a line of force. Actually, the equipotentials and lines of force can only end at charges, stretch to infinity, or double back on themselves in closed loops. The closed-loop pattern is commonly found on the typical topographical contour map which uses roughly parallel lines to represent elevations of terrain. Lines that you sometimes see running at right angles to the contours are lines of maximum slope. The contour map is used to describe many other gradients besides those of altitude. The contours of Figure 45 are actually from a map that depicts variations in gravitational attraction. It could as well show variations in temperature, rainfall, the density of galaxies in the heavens, or some other phenomenon that varies in a continuous manner. Where the lines are close together, the slope or change in variable is steep; where far apart, the change is gradual. If the variable does not change continuously, if it changes abruptly, the lines join or cross one another.

Except for the case of the hole in the plate, the "contours" in Figures 42 and 43 show changes in direction as well as magnitude (the gradients are vectors rather than scalars) but those figures, like Figure 45, represent spatial changes by means of roughly parallel lines. The interesting point is that slopes and gradients are constrained, just like the patterns of more-or-less parallel lines, so that the one mirrors the other.

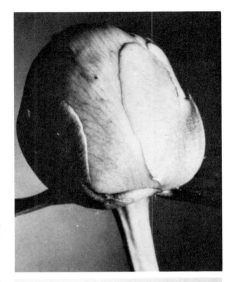

44

45

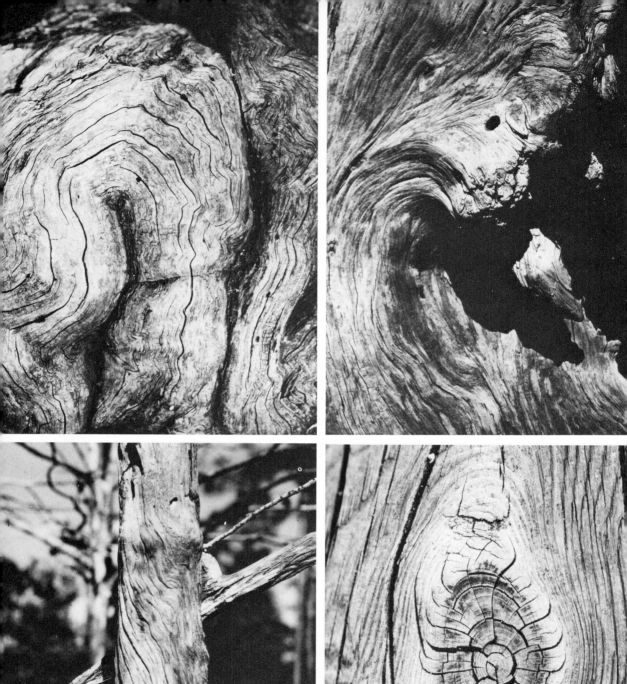

Thus our bundles of lines can flow around obstructions, diverge or converge, extend to infinity, and close on themselves in loops. And, of course, they can make all manner of variations on those arrangements, as modern artists have discovered. But the variations are limited to a few basic types, just like the patterns of force and the mathematical expressions that they describe.

Stress in Wood and Bone

THE SIMILARITY between patterns of streamlines in flowing liquids and patterns of stress in solids explains one of those perplexing questions we frequently encounter in the study of natural form. Why does wood like that shown in the photographs of Figure 46 look turbulent? Does it flow like a liquid? Is it produced by streams and currents? The answer is no. The wood simply grows along lines of stress. It is the stress rather than the wood that "flows."

In this section, we will look at some patterns of stress, and then review what little is known of the mechanisms of growth that allow material to be laid down in those patterns.

To understand how stress is distributed, we should recall the diagram of the beam in bending, shown in Figure 18. The bottom of the beam is stretched in tension while the top is squeezed in compression. Figure 47 shows a similar beam except that instead of carrying a single load in the center, it carries a whole series of loads that are distributed uniformly across its entire length. The figure shows the trajectories of stress within the beam itself. The dotted lines depict trajectories of tension, and the solid lines depict trajectories of compression. We see, at least in the center of the beam, how the lines of tension bunch together at the bottom and the lines of compression bunch together at the top, just as we would expect — the bottom being stretched and the top being compressed. The closeness

of the lines in those bundles at the top and bottom indicate that the stresses are especially high in the center of the beam, again as we would expect, since a beam or column most often fails by bending and breaking in the middle.

In addition, the diagram discloses that the points where the tension and compression trajectories cross lie along a line that runs lengthwise down the center of the beam. Along that line, the so-called neutral axis, tension forces cancel compression forces so that no stress exists. Thus we see why a tubular structure can easily reduce its weight, as an adjunct to increasing its size, by giving up material from its center, from along its neutral axis. Consequently, the hollow quill, the reed, and the straw have about the same strength that they would have if they were solid.

Still, along with a hollow interior, we would expect to see a thickening of the side walls in the middle of the beam or tube where the stresses are most pronounced. As it happens, the human thighbone or femur exhibits just such a thickening. As shown in Figure 48, the femur is essentially a hollow tube. It flares at the top and bottom to receive loads from the pelvis and the knee, and it resists the tendency to buckle or bend by thickening its side walls in the center of its length, exactly where the trajectories of stress are closest together.

48

49

Examination of the top of the femur confirms the fact that new bone actually grows along the stress trajectories. Figure 49 (from Thompson, 1942, after Culmann and Wolff) shows the well-known comparison of the head of the femur with the top of the mast of the Fairbairn crane. D'Arcy Thompson relates that when Karl Culmann, the great German engineer, was busy designing such a crane, he happened to see a similar bone in Hermann Meyer's dissecting room and

saw in a moment that the arrangement of the bony trabeculae was nothing more nor less than a diagram of the lines of stress, or directions of tension and compression, in the loaded structure: in short, that Nature was strengthening the bone in precisely the manner and direction in which strength was required; and he is said to have cried out, "That's my crane!"

From the figure it is clear that the pattern of stress is more complicated for the bone than for the crane, since the top of the bone contains a notch, but the similarity between the two patterns is obvious and both are only complex variations of the pattern of trajectories at the end of the simple beam in Figure 47. Note again in the bone how the solid walls at the sides pick up the lines of stress exactly where they are most consolidated.

The design of bone appears to be beautifully appropriate to its task. It is thick where stress is high, and thin where stress is low. But how does the design come about? How is it actualized? The mechanism is not entirely clear, but presumably tensile and compressive stresses activate pressure-sensitive crystals within the growing material, and those crystals generate electrical fields that align electrically charged molecules and ions. Thus, the "coincidence" of lines of electrical force looking and behaving like lines of stress comes into play, and, through the agency of electrical forces, material gets laid down along lines of stress.

The control of growth in plants and trees is less well understood, but electrical forces may again play a part. However they arise, "turbulent" forms are often materializations of stress. In Figure 50 we see a few leafstalks still attached to the stem of a philodendron, and white scars show where others have fallen away. The dark spot just above the center of the scar marks the position of the central hollow of the leafstalk. The hollowness comes about when the stalk folds around on itself to make a tube. Because the spot is above the center of the scar, we realize that growing material is added to the bottom of the stalk, presumably in response to compressive stress, and that the material serves to prop up the stalk. We see in Figure 51 the bundles of fibers that bandage the trunk of the Indian palm (*Wallichia disticha*, photographed at Fairchild Tropical Gardens in Miami, Florida). We learn from D'Arcy Thompson that those fibers may also develop

50

51

in response to stress. When the trunk bends to any side, the fibers on the opposite side tighten to hold the tree upright.

Stress, Flow, and Engineering

GIVEN THAT STRUCTURAL STRESSES and fluid streamlines often have similar spatial arrangement, it is not surprising that the difficulties that arise in the mathematical analysis of complex engineering structures turn out to be similar to the difficulties of analyzing complicated, i.e., turbulent, flows. Simple structures, like simple flows, are easily described. An eggshell, for example, is easy to analyze. The shell of a crab, however, is not.

A complex form like the shell of a crab has serrated edges, ribbed surfaces, and subtle gradations of thickness. Nature thickens areas of high stress, adds reinforcement between top and bottom plates (see again the horseshoe crab in Figure 19e) and leaves other areas of low stress paper-thin. She responds directly to lines of force without blueprints and mathematics. Man, by contrast, uses forethought: he predicts and quantifies before he builds, since his structures, for the most part, are static and unchanging. Once a man-made structure is erected, the builder or contractor walks away. He does not stay to make continuous modifications in response to changes of temperature, wind, and dynamic loading. Man must therefore make a model of the structure, perhaps with wood and metal, but more likely with mathematics; and that model must enable him to predict accurately whether or not the structure will stand. The difficulty, however, is that we have no general mathematical theory for structural shells. We can only predict the behavior of special shells — shells that are very thin with no abrupt changes in thickness, shells that follow a simple geometrical profile such as a circular dome or a hyperbolic

paraboloid, shells with uniform curvature and uniform loading. Because we must use mathematics, we cannot build as nature builds, freely modifying form and adding material where it is needed, with no attention to a preconceived geometry. Free forms remain, for the most part, beyond our reach. In only a few cases have the constraints of mathematical analysis been bypassed by engineers and architects working directly with models of wire and plaster. Antoni Gaudi's work provides the classic example of building from physical models in an organic manner (Figure 27a above). So, of more recent vintage, does Eero Saarinen's T.W.A. Terminal at New York City's John F. Kennedy Airport (Figure 52).

But our mathematical analysis is improving. That improvement leads to the replacement of simple spheres and cylinders with more complicated organic forms. We note the development of oblate liquid storage tanks that look like drops of water or mercury distorted by gravity (Figure 53). A drop of water is enclosed by a skin of surface tension, and if it sits on a horizontal sheet of glass the water tends to slump within its skin like water in an ice bag. The skin keeps the water from spreading all over the glass, but the drop is changed from a spherical to an oblate form. That squashed shape results in the skin's being stressed equally at all places. To keep the steel skin of a large storage tank stressed equally, it too must be shaped like an ice bag. Thus the engineer has given up

the more easily analyzed and fabricated spherical tank in favor of an oblate tank which distributes stress uniformly. As our mathematical models and fabrication techniques improve, we can expect that man's structures will resemble natural forms even more closely.

4

Spirals, Meanders, and Explosions

Well — yes, the wind does get up and blow out here in West Texas sometimes. Most generally it comes from wherever it happens to be, but the real good hard winds out here come from the north or from the south unless, as happens every once in a while, it gets to going whirligig fashion, and when that happens you might say that things do move.

— FRANK NEFF

Spirals

EDDIES AND WHIRLIGIGS are fascinating things. The eddy appears to be a prototypical model of spatial enclosure. In wrapping around on itself it creates a sheltered and protective environment, a special withinness that is different from the withoutness of the moving stream. It often gets swirled uphill against the current — by the action of the rest of the stream rushing down. It exists by bleeding energy from the mainstream, much like a living thing, for living things also make their environment pay the price for their existence. Through digestion, living things break down the organization of other living things. They leave a trail of broken pieces and disorder in their wake. The universe deteriorates faster because of their existence. But temporarily, as a local organized event, they, like eddies, live and evolve by flowing against the tide.

It is also interesting that eddies so often come in pairs. As we have seen, every stroke of your oar makes a pair of opposite-handed vortexes, and the Kármán vortex street produced by every whistle is lined with both right- and left-handed swirls.

Horns, tusks, and antlers also come in pairs, and each is the mirror image of the other, as if two streams of a viscous fluid flowed in perfect symmetry from openings in the skull (see Figure 62 below). In violation of the rule of double and symmetrical horns are the single horn of the rhinoceros, which is centrally located but is agglutinated hair rather than true horn or bone, and the tusk of the male narwhal, which is an

extreme development of the left front tooth and is asymmetrically placed. The narwhal's tooth grows into a spiral shaft up to nine feet long and may serve as a foil or rapier for ritualized combat during the narwhal's mating season, but it has no other sexual properties — despite being peddled for several centuries as an aphrodisiac derived from the horn of the unicorn. In a few narwhals both front teeth elongate, but, strange to say, both spiral in the same direction, that is to say, they are not mirror images of one another. D'Arcy Thompson suggested that the swimming of the animal imparts a twist to its tusks, but he did not profess certainty in the matter, nor does anyone else.

Except for the tusks of the narwhal, a counterclockwise spiral in horn and bone is usually balanced by a clockwise spiral. Even among leaves we occasionally see the same symmetry. The leaves that curl counterclockwise on the left side of the frond of the sago palm, shown in Figure 54, are opposed by clockwise curls on the right side. Storms spiral counterclockwise above the equator and clockwise below, just as in a more abstract realm, negative numbers camp to the left of zero and positive numbers to the right.

The grasping tendrils of plants also show a balance between opposite curls. As shown in Figure 55*a*, the curl of the tendril moves outward from the stem toward the stick or string or whatever the tendril has grasped, and, at the same time, a curl moves backward from that point of attachment toward the stem. In the middle of the tendril those two oppositely moving curls cancel or neutralize each other in an uncoiled link of vine. As shown in Figure 55*b*, the same straight link can occur in the cord between your telephone and its receiver. To get rid of it, you can dangle the receiver at the end of its cord until the entire length of cord unwinds, that is to say, until it all twists in the same direction.

In a similar sense, Siamese twins also cancel each other. If one twin is right-handed with a clockwise cowlick and has his heart on the left, the other will be left-handed with a counterclockwise cowlick and will have his heart on the right. Siamese twins are thus

enantiomorphs, or mirror images of each other, like right-handed and left-handed crystals. DNA and amino acids come in right- and left-handed forms, and so does sugar (dextrose and levulose), and feeding on the enantiomorphic sugars are enantiomorphic bacteria, with the right-handed bacteria ingesting only the right-handed sugar and the left-handed bacteria eating only left-handed sugar — a little like Jack Sprat and his wife eating the lean and the fat.

The faith that for every right-hand spiral there is a left raises an interesting cosmological question. Physicists have shown that every elementary particle has an enantiomorphic twin, an antiparticle of opposite charge. The neutron is matched by the antineutron, the proton by the antiproton, and the electron by the antielectron or positron. The antiparticles can, in theory, combine to make antielements, antiworlds, and even antilife. If we assume antiparticles to be as numerous as their enantiomorphs, the particles we know — a difficult assumption to avoid since the creation of one type always involves the creation of the other — then we must ask where all the antiparticles have gone. They do not reside with us on earth, since particles and antiparticles annihilate one another in a burst of energy when they come into contact. Have antiparticles made another universe we cannot see? Have they made other galaxies in this universe, or other stars in our own galaxy? Perhaps we see the annihilation of matter and antimatter in the exploding Crab Nebula of Figure 37*h*, or perhaps in the recently discovered and mysteriously energetic quasars.

Perhaps, however, matter and antimatter are not equally plentiful. Maybe the universe is asymmetrical. Nature favors right-handed nucleic acids, alpha helixes, collagen fibers, cilia, and proteins. Those forms all curl clockwise when going away from you, like a conventional wood screw. Why is the clockwise spiral favored? No one knows. Perhaps it was only an evolutionary accident — the right-handed forms happened to make up the organisms that were more fit than their competitors. At a larger scale, forms of life spiral either way: the tendril of the morning glory to the right (opposite to the twist of its blossom, as shown in Figure 56) and the honeysuckle to the left. When they meet they flail about in a hapless tangle. The tendril of the hop turns opposite to the tendril of the vine, so that, as Clerk Maxwell observed, a mirror will transform a beer screw into a wine screw. The coconut palm comes either right or left-handed, although the left-handed variety slightly predominates and reportedly yields more coconuts. The ends of the split tendril of the grape can spiral in either direction. Figure 57 shows two right-handed helixes clutching a stalk of grass. Genes determine the curl of a snail's shell and either the sinistral or dextral form can occur, although in each species one form is more numerous than the other. Figure 58 shows left-handed coiling in the shells of the *Vermicularia spirata*. As Stephen Gould points out, environmental factors that determine whether or not it is advantageous for that snail to reach higher above its

56

57

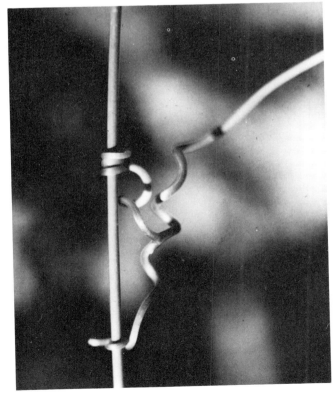

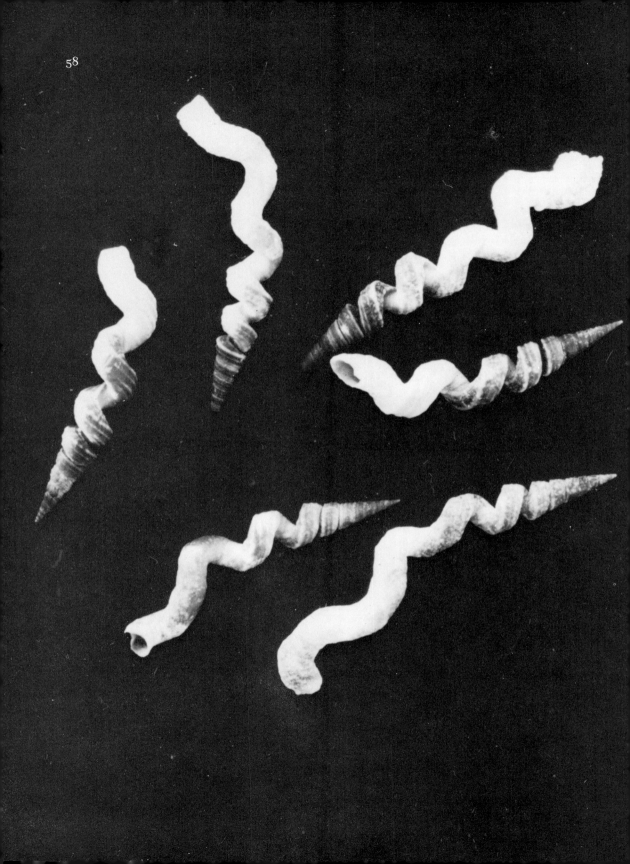

holdfast govern the tightness but not the direction of its coiling.

Quite obviously then, not all spirals come in pairs. Not every cyclone has its anticyclone. You get only one whirlpool when you pull the plug in the bathtub. Have you ever wondered why the center of the vortex in the tub does not fill with water? Interestingly enough, for the same reason that a galaxy has arms. Centrifugal force. The water increases its rotational velocity as it flows to the center of the vortex — just as, once again, the skater whirls faster when he pulls in his arms — because the velocity must increase in order to keep constant the angular momentum. So, as the water flows toward the center of the eddy, it increases its velocity until it spins so fast that it throws itself outward, like a ball on the end of a whirling string. We see the result in Figure 59, where an inner column of air reaches down into the space vacated by the water swirling out of a glass funnel.

59

60

Although all turbulence is characterized by vortexes or spirals, quite obviously, not all spirals are turbulent. The line of Figure 23a, shown earlier, is not a vortex. It is, in its purest form, a simple spiral that maintains a constant distance between successive coils. Since such a spiral was first fully described by Archimedes, it is known by his name. It is the path described by a fly walking outward along the spoke of a revolving wheel. It is the form of a coil of rope, a roll of paper, or in a more complicated version, a ball of string (Figure 60).

The same path is the trail left by the primitive sea slug *Dictyodora*. From studies of its fossil burrows, Adolf Seilacher informs us that the *Dictyodora* once wandered about over the sediments in a haphazard manner, browsing wherever it chose — like a cow in a meadow. But then, through evolution, the *Dictyodora* changed its habits and it came to forage in a tightly wound spiral. The spiral feeding pattern enabled the slug to scour the whole of a given area. Its path was like that of a cow chained to a tree: as the cow wraps the chain around the tree it eats an ever tighter swath through the grass. In the final development of its feeding pattern, the *Dictyodora* moved vertically up and

61

down as it spiraled through the layers of sediment so that its path became a three-dimensional helix or cork-screw.

Many seashells spiral so that the progressively larger domains of the creature wrap around its previous domains in a regular manner (Figure 61). Instead of maintaining the same width as in an Archimedean spiral, the coils of the seashell constantly increase in width to produce what is called a logarithmic or equiangular spiral. As the living creature grows, it extends and enlarges its domain to form a continuous rolled tube, if it is a whelk, or a partitioned tube, if it is the famous chambered nautilus, *Nautilus pompilius*. In both animals each new increment has a similar form and position as the last; it is only a little larger in size. The key to maintaining the spiral growth of the shell is to allow the outer surface, the surface farthest from the axis around which the coiling takes place, to grow more than the inner surface. That difference in growth automatically causes the coiling to take place. Again, no gene need remember or plan the final shape of the shell; it need only facilitate a difference in growth between the inner and outer parts.

As D'Arcy Thompson points out, horns grow in a similar manner. If, at the base of the horn, the leading edge grows more than the trailing edge, the horn curls back. If, at the base, the inside surface which faces the other horn grows more than the outside surface, the horn curls outward. The combination of the two curls, the backward with the outward, results in the helix or corkscrew that we see in the horns of the mountain sheep (Figure 62).

62

The lesson of curvature is quite general and has nothing to do with what tissue or material is involved. Forms curl so that the faster growing or longer surface lies outside and the slower growing or shorter surface lies inside, there being more room outside than inside.

Figure 63 affirms the rule. Rectangular blocks join to make a straight column, but if one of the joining faces of each block is beveled or cut at an angle, the column curls around on itself to make a circle. If the joining

63

face is skewed, that is to say, if the block is cut obliquely, the column curls around on itself to make a three-dimensional helix. In a sense then, the straight column is only a special case of the helix. The straight column is simply a helix with no twist. Now that it has been discovered, we are not surprised to learn that deoxyribonucleic acid or DNA, the material of inheritance in chromosomes, is a combination of two simple helixes, a combination of two columns of sugar and phosphate molecules that twist around on themselves because their edge bonds are of unequal length. Just as the horn results from the deposition of bone in oblique layers, the double helix of the DNA results from the stacking of skewed molecular units.

That one principle, that the longer surface is outside the shorter surface, is common to all spirals. The longer streamline is outside of and curls around the shorter streamline, and the stretched lower surface of the loaded beam wraps around the compressed upper surface. Your automobile is equipped with differential gears which allow the rear wheel on the outside of the curve to rotate faster and cover more distance than the rear wheel on the inside of the curve.

Thermostats operate on the same principle. If, as shown in Figure 64, strips of brass and iron of the same length (top) are heated separately (middle), the brass (light-colored strip) expands more than the iron. If the strips are joined and then heated, the brass strip curls around the iron strip (bottom). The curling and uncurling of the two strips together turns your furnace off and on.

The general rule is clear. If the rates of growth or expansion of two surfaces are equal, the material lies straight. If the rates are unequal, the material curls so that the slower growing surface is inside the faster growing surface. We see manifestations of the rule everywhere we look. Figure 65 shows curls of peeling paint, modified leaves around the pistil of a water lily, a dried leaf from a poinsettia, and the warped surface of a dying leaf just before it falls from the tree. In all those examples the longer surface wraps around and encloses the shorter surface. The same is true in the

turning outward of the human lip as the inner tissue grows faster than the outer tissue, and even in the bending of our arms and legs when the muscles on one side contract and the muscles on the other relax. All confirm that short surfaces are enclosed by long ones, that more space exists outside a given area than inside.

Meanders

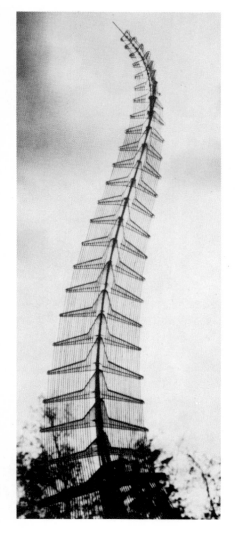

The way of a snake upon a rock is beyond understanding.
—Proverbs 30:19

THE MEANDER is closely related to the spiral. We have seen in a growing thing that if one surface is longer than another, the form curves around on itself. If the growth of two different surfaces varies in a periodic manner, the form weaves back and forth in a meander. The muscles of a snake, for example, alternately tighten and relax in cycles along each side. Those alternating contractions and extensions force its body to undulate to and fro, just as our muscles control the variable shape of our backbones, and wires govern the shape of Frei Otto's flexible column (Figure 66). In Otto's design, triangular plates decreasing in size toward the top of the column carry compressional loads. They are like the vertebrae of our backbones. Tension wires terminate at the different plates, and when those wires are shortened or lengthened by means of a control device at the base, the column quickly turns or bends in any direction. Whatever its shape, the flexible column, again like our backbones, can carry superimposed loads.

In the same way that the Archimedean spiral wraps around itself to fill space, the random meander twists and turns and doubles back on itself so that it too fills space. Figure 23*b* in chapter 2 shows how. The brain coral and the magnetic domains of garnet in Figure 67 have the same pattern. In both forms, close-packed meanders arise from competitive struggle. The coral polyps, the living creatures with tiny waving tentacles, line the valleys of the brain coral in soldierly rows. They pile up their excrement on the ridges between the valleys like sandbags on a levee, and each row pushes and gets pushed by the neighboring rows through the intermediary of the ridges. Each row advances or retreats as the relentless pressure of the others dictates. The result is an equilibrium pattern of close-packed meanders. In the garnet, the rows of north and south magnetic polarities similarly jockey for territory.

But then, what about the single meandering line, the line of the river, for instance, whose form is not a product of the pushing and pulling of neighboring streams? Why does the river flow in its chosen pattern?

At first we might suppose that the river follows the terrain, that it twists and bends in direct response to peaks and dips in the landscape. Extreme slopes, of course, do dictate the direction of flow of a river, but on a smooth and gentle slope, we find that water does not flow straight downhill; it wanders back and forth like a skier running a slalom. It winds and turns in a quiet but seemingly desperate manner to avoid the straight schuss to the bottom. Furthermore, the windings turn out to be surprisingly regular, quite independent of subtle changes in topography. The bends are predictable. They are not circular arcs, parabolic arcs, or sine curves; they are elliptic integrals and they have the exceptional characteristic of being the smoothest of curves, of having the least change in the direction of their curvature.

Those regular curves occur in big rivers and in small. For instance, Figure 68 (redrawn from Leopold, 1960), shows three streams: Duck Creek near Cora, Wyoming, the New Fork River near Pinedale, Wyoming, and the Mississippi River at Point Breeze, Louisiana, with widths of eight feet, sixty feet and thirty-four hundred feet. Despite variations in width of over four hundred to one, all three streams flow in the same meander pattern. All three streams have the same proportions.

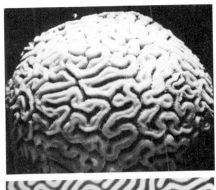

67

68

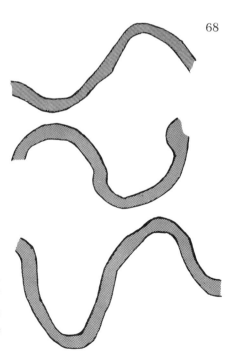

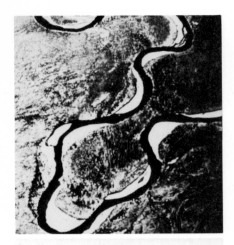

69

70

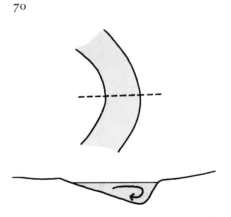

From studies of over fifty rivers, the hydrologist Luna B. Leopold reports that no river, whatever its size, runs straight for more than ten times its width. Moreover, the radius of a bend is nearly always two to three times the width, and the wavelength — the distance between analogous points of analogous bends — is seven to ten times the width. Thus, despite dramatic variations in size and bed conditions, rivers run a strikingly uniform course. Figure 69 shows similar meanders in a river in Alaska and the Snake River in Wyoming.

We have three different explanations for the occurrence of the regular meander pattern. We have three different models to explain why nearly all rivers and streams wind in the same way.

The first is the mechanical model, and interestingly enough, it was nicely described by Albert Einstein. Einstein's explanation involves once again the effect of centrifugal force. If we assume that a small bend of a river comes into being owing to some minor irregularity of terrain, the centrifugal force that arises as the water goes around the bend tends to fling the water outward toward the concave bank. (To counteract an analogous outward movement, racetracks are designed with banked turns.) Because the water at the top surface of a river is slowed less by the friction of the banks, it moves across the stream toward the concave bank and is replaced from below by water that moves across the bottom of the stream in the opposite direction. Consequently, as diagrammed in Figure 70, a circular current is established that, at the surface, drives toward the concave bank, dives at and scours the bank, then reverses direction and slowly rises, retarded by friction along the bottom. The cross section of the stream becomes asymmetrical, as shown in the figure, and, more importantly, the concave bank is eroded so as to increase the curvature or sharpness of the bend. Increasing the curvature of the bend throws the river into a path that traverses the hill rather than coursing straight down. Eventually, however, gravity pulls the river around into a downhill path, creating another bend and another circulation in cross section, but this time a bend and a circulation that are opposite in direction to the first. The new bend increases its curvature as a result of its centrifugal force and the stream, instead of continuing to flow straight down the hill, traverses the hill in the other direction. Thus the process continues. Scour increases the curvature of each bend so that the stream must continually correct itself like a driver steering a little to the left and then to the right and back again to the left as he travels down the highway.

It is of interest to note that owing to the general forward flow of the water, the point of maximum scour is just a little forward or a little downhill of the apex of the bend. The scour thus leads the bend further downstream. In fact, all the bends, more or less in unison, move downstream. The farmer with land at the bend of the river sees over the years only his local bend and thinks of it as fickle, turning one way and then the other, depositing fresh soil and then eating soil away. The more correct view, however, is that he inherits his neighbor's bend from up the river and then still other bends beyond that.

The second way to describe meanders is in terms of a uniform expenditure of energy. The scour makes the bends smooth and uniform with no sharp changes in direction. That smoothness minimizes erosion so that the river does as little work or gives up as little energy going around the bends as is possible. A flexible metal strip like the shutter-release cable of Figure 71 also avoids concentrated bends, and its uniform curves imitate quite well the meanders of rivers. So does a fireman's hose, a boa constrictor, the path of a pedestrian (as well as a skier), and so should our highways if we are to avoid lurches, skids, and sudden braking.

The river then seems interested in giving up its energy in as uniform a manner as possible. In the straight shallow reaches it gives up energy by generating heat in ripples and rapids. In the deep and quiet pools, where the going is easy, it twists itself into a bend, as if to expend the same energy there that it does in the reaches. Thus, a river seems to pace itself in its work. It bends or goes out of its way in order to

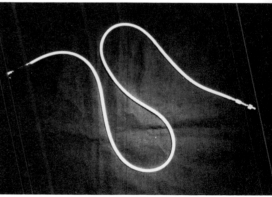

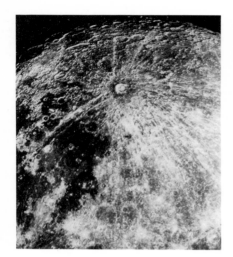

72

73

keep its work uniform, to expend the same amount of energy everywhere, in the quiet deeps as well as in the rippling shallows.

The third model for meanders comes from analyzing the lines of a river in terms of randomness and probability. Hermann von Schelling of the General Electric Company has proved the general rule that any line of fixed length that stretches between two fixed points is likely to follow a meander. He mathematically generated random walks or paths in which a moving point can strike off in any direction as it journeys between two fixed appointments, as long as the total length of its trip comes out right. He found that the most probable path for such a moving point is a serpentine pattern with proportions similar to those found for rivers.

In order to describe meanders, then, we can invoke a model involving scour and centrifugal force, a model that describes the uniform expenditure of energy, or a model based on probability theory. All three models describe the same phenomenon. As far as meanders are concerned, all three models happen to be interrelated — but not out of any fundamental necessity. That is to say, the cross circulation induced by centrifugal force need not *necessarily* result in a uniform distribution of effort or produce a path that is especially probable. In a world of limited patterns, however, the meander answers several entirely different sets of specifications, so that scour, uniform effort, and probability produce the same design.

Explosions

ANOTHER PATTERN, in some ways related to flow, is the explosion. It is especially easy to identify and understand. As was shown in Figure 24, the pattern is characterized by direct paths from the center to every outlying point, so that the density of the paths falls off with distance from the origin — like the intensity of sound and light.

In Figure 72 we see the pattern in the crater of Tycho on the moon where material has been splashed fifteen hundred miles in all directions. The farther you go from the central crater, the fewer and more spread-out are the rays. In Figure 73 we observe the pattern in three-dimensional space in a bursting firecracker, and again the density of material decreases at increasing distances from the burst.

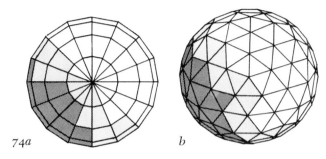

74a   b

When the explosive pattern is used in man-made structures, the concentration of material at the center often results in overdesign. Less material can be used in the design of a dome, for example, when the ribs are distributed in a geodesic rather than an explosive pattern. Figure 74 shows how the ribs of a conventional dome radiate outward and downward in an explosive pattern. The greatest concentration of material is in the center and at the top of the dome — just where the loads are the lightest. By way of contrast, the geodesic dome (b) has a uniform distribution of ribs with no excessive concentrations of material. With only a little strengthening of the ribs at the bottom of the dome, as described previously, the geodesic pattern nicely fits the distribution of stress.

Figure 75 shows a linear explosion in which an ink-soaked string is pinned at its ends and snapped in its middle against a piece of paper so that it leaves a long linear splatter. The pattern is a linear variation of the circular splashes of Figure 77 below and it reminds us of the spiky bottlebrush flower of Figure 76. Such a

75

76

77

spattering of ink reveals much about the formation of the explosion pattern, particularly the way in which the pattern is affected by scale.

By way of explanation, Figure 77 shows the spatter of drops of ink released from four different heights. Reading from the top, we see imprints of drops that have been released from an eyedropper at heights of three inches, six inches, twelve inches, and twenty-four inches — each height being double the preceding one. The diameter of the splash does not double or even increase by $\sqrt{2}$ as we would expect if the linear dimensions or areas of one splash were twice those of another. Instead, the diameters increase more slowly and the splashes generate regular spikes, first as slight undulations in the perimeter, then as small bumps and knobs, and finally as developed spines. As a response to being dropped with different velocities, the splashes change their form.

Dropping the ink from a still greater height does not appreciably increase the length of the trajectories, since the drop cannot overcome air resistance and fall faster. An ink-soaked tissue, moving at higher velocity, produces very long streaks when it splashes (Figure 78).

For another example, observe Figure 79. Taken at 1/10,000 of a second, that photograph by Harold E. Edgerton shows a drop of milk as it splashes from a height of about seven inches onto a plate covered with a thin layer of milk. Note the beautiful regularity of the spikes.

The biologist Paul Weiss has made some far-reaching observations on the shapes of those drops and splashes. A spike originates at a weak point in the perimeter of the splash and liquid flowing up a spike sucks more liquid into its stream, so that new spikes cannot get started in the vicinity of one already existing. Here, Weiss points out, lies an important principle: an area of existing growth prevents areas of new growth from starting nearby, and, even more comprehensively, a general stimulant to growth favors areas that grow fast, like the spikes, at the expense of those that grow slow, like the areas between the spikes. Weiss reports

that just as dropping the ink from a greater height stimulates the growth of spikes at the expense of the rest of the perimeter, "higher temperature promotes the growth of limbs, tails, gills, etc., more than that of the bulk of the body; the snout, legs, and tails of rats and mice raised in warmth are not only absolutely but also relatively longer in proportion to the body than those of specimens raised in the cold."

Thus, as the inkblot increases its size in response to an increase in the velocity of its fall, it changes its form: it adds spikes around its perimeter in a regular manner. So too with living forms. As they increase their size in response to their environment, they also change their form: they also increase their perimeters or surfaces in a regular manner.

The pattern of the explosion is really the first of our branching patterns. It represents a form of branching that is efficient in the sense that it is direct, but is

80

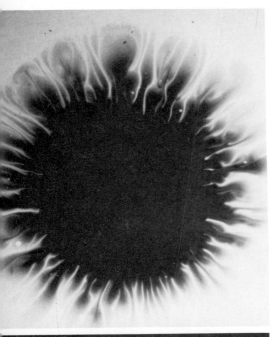

81a

b

inefficient in its failure to minimize the total length of network. A simple explosive form is seen in the thistle of Figure 80 in which a uniform distribution of little spikes increases the surface area.

Figure 81 shows more complex examples. In Figure 81a, ink dropped into glycerin diffuses outward to form wavy tentacles. The shape of the drop comes about through the formation of an interface between the ink and the glycerin that is stable, at least temporarily. The small difference in density between the ink and the glycerin behaves like that between the sea anemone in b (which is composed mostly of water) and the water itself. The interface between the anemone and the water is brought about genetically or by some other means — not necessarily by diffusion as with the ink. Consequently the sea anemone and inkdrop are similar in form because they are expressions of equilibrium between two "fluids" of slightly different density — not because they necessarily arise from a similar mechanism of growth.

The trajectories of the explosion may terminate in explosions of their own, the way streamers of the rocket burst on the fourth of July end in a barrage of smaller bursts, or material ejected from a large crater flies across the surface of the moon to make secondary craters. The prototype of that compound explosion is Figure 25a and, as we have seen, although it is a little indirect in comparison with the single explosive burst — although some of the paths to some of the points are longer than in the simple pattern — it has appreciably less total path; it uses significantly less length of line to join its parts.

As Figures 82, 83, and 84 indicate, many plants and flowers grow in the pattern of the compound explosion. Figure 82 shows the head of an aralia (*Aralia hispida*) that looks like a succession of rocket bursts. Each branch in each cluster breaks into a cluster of its own. We see the same design in the spiraea, where each branch ramifies to form a calix and petals. Those ramifications are particularly apparent when we view the cluster from the rear.

In the *Bismarckia nobilis* of Figure 83 (photographed

82

83

at the Fairchild Tropical Gardens in Miami, Florida), the leaflets of the frond spring from a common center, as do the fronds themselves.

The dandelion has the same design. In frame *a* of Figure 84 we see an open flower and a bud. Frame *b* shows a cross section through the bud with all the petals stacked in readiness for the grand opening. Next we see the flower after the petals have withered and died *c*. Their remains are visible at the top. Below the petals are the developing tufts of seeds. When fully open, the tufts form a delicate sphere ready for a child to blow (*d, e*). In the last frame we see a single attached seed, the rest having been blown away. The seed repeats the design of the whole: it branches into a tuft of down just as the entire stem branches into a tuft of petals.

84a

5

Models of Branching

I N CHAPTER 2 we found that geometrical properties in abstract patterns of lines and dots frequently aid our understanding of natural form. In this chapter we will develop a few more abstract patterns. Some readers may find the study of generalized patterns tedious and will want to push on to the examples from nature described in the next chapter, but the idea behind the abstract models is an exciting one. The idea is this: abstract patterns, whether developed through doodles, fine art, or mathematical analysis, are those that nature develops through the interaction of physical systems. All patterns, whether drawn by artists, calculated by mathematicians, or produced by natural forces are shaped by the same spatial environment. All are subject to the tyranny of space. Synthetic patterns of lines and dots are engaging in their own right but, more importantly, they speak eloquently of the order that all things inevitably share.

Here are some questions that our models can answer. Trees have a few large branches that split into many small ones: what is the order of those branches? How big are the limbs and boughs in relation to the sprigs and twigs? And why do streams and discharges of lightning branch like trees? Why do so many systems extend themselves by adding smaller and smaller parts?

Random Branching
of Rivers and Trees

HERE IS ANOTHER QUESTION. When rain falls uniformly on gently sloping terrain, what kind of a network of streams will emerge?

That question cannot be given a precise answer because many factors influence the direction of flow within a stream network — topography, vegetation, variation in rainfall, lithology, centrifugal force at the bends of streams — and those factors interact with one another in a complicated fashion. But although we cannot predict the exact network that will develop, we are not entirely frustrated. If we assume that the direction of flow at different points is randomly determined — just as we did for velocities in a turbulent flow — we can describe the general characteristics of the network. Even more to the point, we can obtain general descriptions of stream networks by generating artificial patterns of flow.

For example, if we draw a mosaic of equal hexagons and then use a set of random numbers (such as the digits of pi) to determine the directions of flow inside the hexagons, most of those randomly determined flows will link up automatically to form a branched network.

Figure 85 shows networks generated in that manner. Actually, for the sake of clarity, the figure shows only a few of the hexagonal cells and only the first few digits of pi. Other cells and digits are used to generate the complete pattern, however, and all cells are interconnected with branching lines according to the following rule: if the digit within a cell is even, the center of the cell joins the center of the cell below and to the right; if the digit is odd, the center joins the cell below and to the left. The resulting branching pattern can be extended indefinitely in any direction by using more digits in a larger array. Although details within the larger pattern would differ from those shown in the figure, the general appearance would be about the same. Figure 86 shows the largest unified network or tree that is embedded in the pattern of Figure 85.

Figure 87 shows a slightly different interconnection of the cells. The digits are placed as before and the same rule is used, but the connecting lines run along the perimeters of the cells rather than through their centers. Again, Figure 88 shows the largest tree that can be extracted from the pattern. Topologically, with regard to numbers of points, lines, and junctions, that tree is identical to the tree in Figure 86, although visually, since angles and lengths of lines are different, it looks quite different.

When Luna B. Leopold generated branching patterns from random numbers, he found that the patterns resembled natural river systems. Although our patterns have not been generated in exactly the same manner as his, let us see if they too are similar to rivers. In order to make the comparison, we will perform a "Horton analysis" of the patterns — the classic method of analyzing river systems, first used by the engineer Robert E. Horton (and subsequently modified by A. N. Strahler).

The analysis splits a stream system into first-, second-, third-, etc., order streams according to the rule that a higher-order stream can be fed only by lower-order streams. Thus, a first-order stream, which originates at a source, receives no other streams, a second-order stream, which originates at the junction of two first-order streams, receives only first-order streams, a third-order stream, which originates at the junction of two second-order streams, receives only second- and first-order streams, and so forth. In actual river basins, streams of one order turn out to be three to five times as numerous as streams of the next higher order. In other words, in a given network, first-order streams are about four times as common as second-order streams which in turn are about four times as common as third-order streams. How do our randomly generated patterns compare with those statistics?

If in Figure 89 we redraw Figure 86 and represent first-order branches, which have no tributaries, by lines marked with a single dot, second-order branches, which start at the junction of two first-order branches, by lines marked with two dots, and so forth, we find

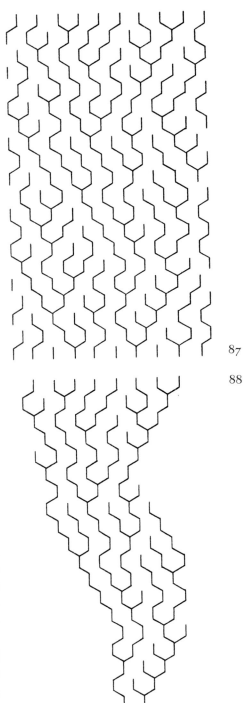

87

88

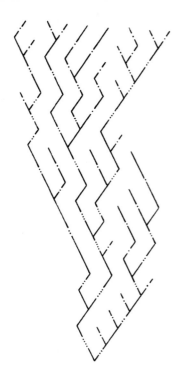

twenty-four first-order branches, six second-order branches, and two third-order branches, showing, just as Horton observed for natural streams, that the branches of each order are three to five times as numerous as the branches of the next higher order. An analysis of the network or tree in Figure 88 gives the same bifurcation ratios since it forks in the same manner.

We recognize another formal tendency in the pattern of Figure 89: streams of higher order tend to be longer than those of lower order. That tendency is also found in rivers. It allows hydrologists to estimate the total lengths of all streams in a basin once they have determined the number of orders in the basin. Based on such an estimate, they posit the existence of 3,250,000 miles of river channel in the United States.

Horton found that drainage area too is related to stream order, and that the length of a river's main channel L is, on the average, 1.4 times the drainage area A raised to a power. The exponent runs around two-thirds. As a formula, then,

$$L = 1.4A^{\frac{2}{3}}$$

In actual river basins, the factor 1.4 varies between 1 and 2.5 and the exponent varies between 0.6 and 0.7. Within those limits, the branching pattern of Figure 89 also follows the formula.

The exponent two-thirds in the empirical formula reveals still more about the shape of rivers. If the exponent was one-half, that is to say, if the length of the river system was proportional to the square root of the drainage area, the shape of river basins would be the same for both large and small rivers. An exponent larger than one-half, such as two-thirds, indicates instead that the basin of a large river tends to be long and narrow while the basin of a small river tends to be short and fat. Thus we find that a change in size is accompanied by a change in shape. Interestingly, the irrigation systems in leaves show a similar tendency, namely, the larger leaves tend to be more elongated. The large elongated leaf of the banana stands in contrast to the small rounded leaf of the blueberry.

If we were to make very large arrays of hexagons and interconnect them according to our rule, the bifurcation ratios and relations between length and area would not precisely imitate natural streams. Synthetic patterns, in which flow has only two choices (to move downward at a constant angle either to the right or to the left), grow too long and narrow; they do not spread enough in width. Real streams in real networks are confronted by more than two choices. Nevertheless, we still find it true that the pattern of Figure 89 looks superficially and acts statistically like a small river basin.

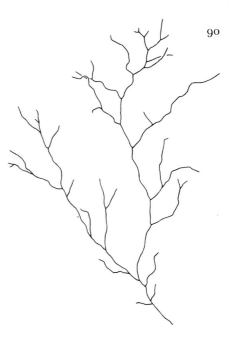

90

Figure 90 is a tracing of a photograph of a stroke of lightning. The actual stroke is, of course, three-dimensional, but a "Horton analysis" of its two-dimensional projection in the figure reveals the same bifurcation ratios we find in a river system. Specifically, we find in the lightning 33 first-order branches, 10 second-order branches, and 2 third-order branches. The ratio between first and second orders and the ratio between second and third orders are thus 3.3 and 5.0 — within the expected range of 3 to 5. Our sample is too small to enable us to make a definitive statement about the similarity of patterns in lightning and rivers; however, investigators like Michael Woldenberg are extending that kind of analysis. Woldenberg has determined bifurcation ratios and other statistical parameters in human lungs, cows' livers, economic market areas, streams, and electrical discharges (like those in Figure 91). In all those diverse systems he finds similar hierarchies of stream orders.

The lichtenberg figures of Figure 91 are formed when blocks of plastic are charged with static electricity and their surface ruptured at one point. The electricity flows out with a rush and leaves behind beautiful branched networks. The pattern in *a* was obtained by pricking the bottom edge of the plastic block; the pattern in *b* by pricking the front surface. Statistically, with regard to stream orders, those patterns are similar to networks of rivers.

Without going into analytical detail, we thus discover that many very different things branch in similar

91a

b

fashion. Again and again, branches of low order turn out to be shorter and more numerous than branches of high order.

We begin to suspect, then, that Horton's statistical findings depend more on the general properties of space than on the mechanism of flow in actual streams. Similar patterns in tributaries, lungs, lightning discharges, and randomly generated networks do not arise because of similarities of materials or forces — water is not the same as lung tissue, nor is electricity the same as liver. The resemblances arise because in each of those systems the field of action, the spatial arena, is the same.

If any network is to be distributed uniformly in space, it must fan out at the periphery — in direct response to the way space itself fans out. In a branching network, that fanning out manifests itself in the development of a large number of little streams. The network grows by the extension of some of those small streams, but those extended streams also fan or feather out to develop streams of their own. Thus a hierarchy of branches develops in which the small ones always outnumber the large ones.

Topology of Random Branching

THE TOPOLOGICAL RELATIONS in branching patterns also show how the spatial environment determines the pattern. At the end of Chapter 2 we discovered that many different patterns can be described by the formula

$$1 J_1 \pm 0 J_2 - 1 J_3 - 2 J_4 - \ldots = 2$$

where $J_1, J_2, \ldots$, are the number of one-way, two-way, etc., junctions. We can use the same formula to describe random branching patterns. That description is made easy by two facts: forks or junctions seldom exist at which more than three lines meet; and two-way junctions do not change the total value of the formula. Thus, for patterns of random branching, we need consider only the number of one-and three-way junctions. Accordingly, our formula reduces to

$$J_1 - J_3 = 2$$

The number of one-way joints J_1 is simply the number of sources plus the exit; thus it is equal to the number of first-order streams plus one. The number of three-way joints J_3 is the number of triple junctions in the interior of the network.

Now, in order to see the consequence of the formula, let us imagine a stream fed by five sources. What possible configurations can it have? We know it will have five first-order streams, and since $J_1 = 5 + 1 = J_3 + 2$, the number of triple junctions J_3 equals 4. Similarly, if we had a tributary system with 100 sources, we would inevitably find 100 first-order streams and 99 triple junctions.

But how are the triple junctions distributed? How many second-order, third-order, etc., streams exist in a given network? In a classic paper published in 1966, Ronald L. Shreve discovered the answer.

From Shreve's analysis we can describe the simple case of a stream system that has five sources. As Figure 92 shows, the sources can be distributed in fourteen different ways. Each of the fourteen networks is distinct in the sense that no amount of stretching or twisting will transform one into another. Each of the configurations has four three-way joints as predicted by our formula. Now Shreve's insight was to say that each of the fourteen possible networks has an equal chance of being adopted by an actual five-source stream that flows across uniform terrain. Of the fourteen possibilities, the eight at the top of the figure have 5 first-order streams and 1 second-order stream, whereas the six at the bottom have 5 first-order streams, 2 second-order streams, and 1 third-order stream. Since, according to Shreve, each distinct network is equally possible in the natural landscape, we should find that, in eight out of fourteen cases, five-source streams have 5 and 1 first-and second-order streams, and that, in six out of four-

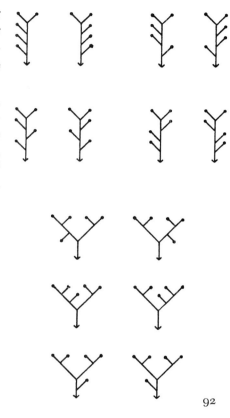

92

teen cases, they have 5, 2, and 1 first-, second-, and third-order streams. Networks of actual five-source streams bear out the prediction.

The number of possible networks increases rapidly with an increase in the number of sources. There are $2,275 \times 10^{56}$ different networks for a stream with one hundred sources! But whatever the number of sources, the number of different networks is finite, and when all the possibilities are considered (as can be done with a computer) the ratio of stream orders that is most likely to occur seems to be the one that we find in nature. Horton's empirical discovery that the streams of one order are three to five times as numerous as those of the next higher order describes the bifurcation ratios of streams in the vast majority of possible networks. Specific forces in the landscape interact with one another in such a multitude of ways that the properties of stream networks in nature turn out to be just those of the average case; natural networks have exactly those features that are shared by the majority of all possible networks.

Least Work and Angles of Branching

DESPITE STATISTICAL PROOF of the correspondence between our branching patterns and rivers, Figure 86 does not really look like a river, nor does Figure 88 come much closer. The forks in those patterns are too abrupt and regular. The branches do not flow gracefully into one another.

In order to determine the proper angle at each fork or intersection, we must now concern ourselves with the actual forces of flow. In particular, we will do well to review the work of Cecil D. Murray who showed how considerations of least effort describe the branching angles of arteries.

Forewarned that the principle of least work involves some mathematical reasoning, since, in the last

analysis, work is a mathematical concept, let us suppose in Figure 93 that blood travels in a main artery
from A to point D. Now, suppose that some blood also
reaches point P through a side branch. If blood flows
directly from B to P, it travels within a small artery
with its large frictional loss over a long distance. The
work of the blood traversing that route is

$$F_{BP} \times BP$$

that is to say, the force F_{BP} required to drive blood
through the narrow side branch times the length of
that branch BP. Alternatively, the blood could proceed
from B to C in the large artery with its small frictional
loss and then cross over to point P. In that alternate
route the total work is

$$(F_{BC} \times BC) + (F_{CP} \times CP)$$

that is to say, the force F_{BC} required to drive blood
through the main artery times the length of the main
artery BC, plus the force F_{CP} required to drive blood
through the branch artery times the length of that
branch CP.

Which of those two routes involves less work? It is
difficult to say, for the answer depends on the relative
sizes of the main and branch arteries. The first route is
shorter, but the blood travels a longer distance in the
constricted branch where the going is difficult; the
second route is longer but the blood travels a shorter
distance in the constricted branch. Perhaps an intermediate route, with a branch striking off somewhere
between points B and C, would involve less work than
either of the others. Perhaps some intermediate route
would involve the least possible work, that is to say,
would minimize the sum of the products of forces and
lengths. If so, blood will travel that route.

Thinking about the choice of routes for a moment,
we would expect, as Wilhelm Roux observed, that if
the main artery is very large in comparison with the
branch artery, blood will flow with less effort if it
travels primarily in the large artery and minimizes its
journey in the small, that is, if the small artery splits off
from the main artery at close to a 90-degree angle. On

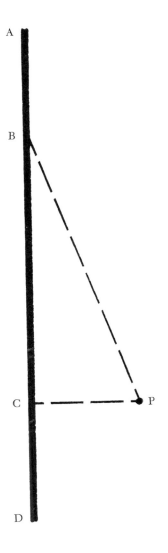

93

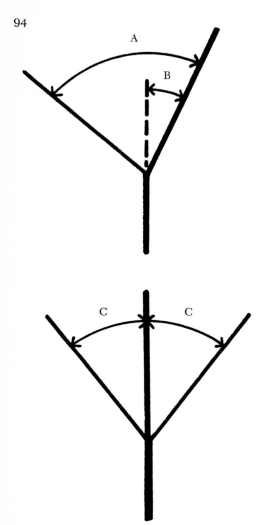

the other hand, if the main and branch arteries are close to the same size, blood will, with no increase in effort, switch over to the branch, and, as Roux again observed, large branches will strike off from main arteries at angles considerably narrower than 90 degrees. We can thus frame a general rule: the smaller the branch, the closer to 90 degrees will be its angle of divergence from the trunk.

Let us see how Murray made Roux's observations quantitative. From considerations of least work, Murray developed a system, shown in Figure 94 and the graph of Figure 95 which makes straightforward the whole business of determining angles of branching.

To use the graph, simply enter the ratio between the diameters of two branches and note the angle listed at the left. Use the top curve for angle A between the branch and the extension of the trunk, the bottom curve for angle B for the deflection of the trunk, and the middle curve for angle C between either of two equal branches and the extension of the trunk. Figure 94 shows those angles.

Note that two equal branches that diverge from the main artery or trunk directly opposite one another do not deflect the trunk, whereas one branch deflects the trunk through an angle B — in agreement with Leonardo da Vinci's observation:

> The branches of plants are found in two different positions: either opposite to each other or not opposite. If they are opposite to each other the center stem is not bent; if they are not opposite the center stem is bent.

Examining some more implications of Murray's graph, we see that the curve that describes angle A between the trunk and a branch is relatively flat, that is to say, the angle between two adjacent branches shows little variation for branches of different size. If a trunk bifurcates into two equal branches, with the ratio between their diameters equal to one, they diverge by about 75°. If the bifurcation produces small branches — with a ratio of diameter of branch to the

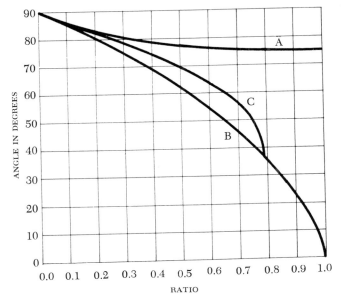

95

diameter of extension of trunk approaching zero — the divergence is close to 90°. Branching angles thus vary within the narrow range of 75° to 90°. However, angle B, the deflection of the trunk, varies from 0° for small branches to 90° for large branches. Those relations are just what Roux observed: the small branch diverges from the trunk at close to 90° and disturbs the line of the trunk but little; the large branch diverges less from the line of the trunk but disturbs the trunk more.

Another observation made by Leonardo da Vinci turns out not to be confirmed by Murray's finding. Leonardo said:

> All the branches of trees at every stage of their height, united together, are equal to the thickness of their trunk.

Mathematically then, we might expect the cross-sectional area of the trunk to equal the cross-sectional area of the branches, so that when a trunk with diameter d_0 splits into two branches with diameters d_1 and d_2,

$$d_0{}^2 = d_1{}^2 + d_2{}^2$$

In the derivation of his formulas, however, Murray

assumed something quite different. He supposed that volumes rather than cross-sectional areas are equal, that

$$d_0{}^3 = d_1{}^3 + d_2{}^3$$

Murray's supposition is that the cross-sectional area of the branches is larger than that of the trunk, that the branches have more room for the passage of fluid than the trunk that feeds them. D'Arcy Thompson makes clear the reason for Murray's assumption. Thompson tells us to consider resistance to flow rather than capacity for flow, and since the branches offer more resistance to flow than the trunk, their cross-sectional area must be increased if they are to transport the same amount of fluid.

By how much should the area of the branches exceed the area of the trunk? Murray assumed that for equality of transport the diameters of trunk and branches should be cubed, that their exponent should be three; but later, when he measured weights of tree limbs and observed their branching angles, he found an exponent of about 2.5. That lower exponent correlates with the finding that the angle between two equal branches in a tree is closer to 60° than the 75° found in an artery. We might assume that the narrow forks of trees make the limbs easier to support against the forces of gravity. Still, even in trees, the exponent is larger than two. Hence, Leonardo's observation must be modified, for all branches united together exceed rather than equal the thickness of the trunk.

Just as trees branch with angles slightly different from arteries, so too, most probably, do rivers and strokes of lightning. But in all such systems of flow, be the vehicle blood, water, or electrons, Roux's observations still hold: small branches make large angles with the trunk and deflect it a small amount; large branches make small angles with the trunk but deflect it greatly.

Let us see what happens if we use Murray's graph to establish the angles of the branches in the pattern of Figure 86. We can assume that the lines of the pattern represent channels of flow and that the greater the number of hexagonal cells a channel connects, that is to say, the larger the area that it "drains," the greater will be its width. In order to compensate for the proportionately greater frictional losses that occur in small channels, we will use Murray's assumption of a cube exponent and set the cube of the diameter of each branch proportional to the number of hexagonal cells it traverses. We can thus determine the diameters of the branches, enter their ratios in the graph of Figure 95, and obtain the pattern of Figure 96.

That tree is topologically identical to the tree of Figure 86 from which it is derived. Both trees have 24 first-order branches and 23 triple junctions arranged in

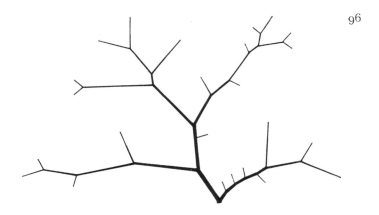

96

precisely the same hierarchical sequence. Note, however, that the modification of the pattern on the basis of least effort — on the basis of the forces involved in flow — creates a pattern that looks a good deal like the branch of a real tree.

It is especially interesting that Figure 96 was drawn with no concern for the appearance of a real tree. The lengths of its branches and its topological characteristics were generated from random numbers whereas the angles and thicknesses of its branches were generated from a theoretical model of least work. The angles between branches may be a little large (we assumed an exponent of 3 rather than 2.5) and the branches may seem a little stiff and straight, but using only mathe-

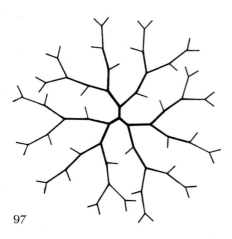

97

matical models we have made a form that is surprisingly organic in appearance.

Figure 97 shows another pattern developed with the aid of Murray's graph. That figure is a transformation of Figure 26, the branching pattern that connects points in a hexagonal array with the least length of line. The transformation, Figure 97, looks like an aerial view of a tree in winter. The minimum network with its angles of 120° becomes a network with angles that vary from 75° to 90°, as dictated by the relative lengths of its branches. The generalized network of minimum length becomes, through considerations of the specific forces at each junction, a network of minimum work in which frictional resistance as well as length plays a part.

We should take special note of the intimate relations among the branches of the patterns in Figures 96 and 97. For example, if any branch is doubled in length, its diameter becomes $\sqrt[3]{2}$ or 1.26 times as large. That increase in diameter affects the ratio of the diameters at the nearest fork, and, to a lesser extent, the ratios at all the other forks down to the roots. The angles of all those forks make small compensatory adjustments in accordance with Murray's graph, so that, like a living tree, the artificial tree responds to subtle changes in its parts, or, in the words of Viollet-le-Duc, "every detail bears a defined relation to the general composition."

This section calls for a parenthetical remark about the difference between the model and the thing that is modeled. The principle of least work can easily mislead us into supposing that nature builds trees or blood vessels according to teleologic principle, according to an overall scheme of far-sighted economy. We have assumed in our example of the artery that nature decides to move blood from a trunk to some specific point P and then chooses the best route to accomplish the task. In reality, however, no blood need ever arrive at point P; that it does arrive there is because the angle of divergence between the artery and the branch allowed it to, that angle being determined by the play of forces at the point of divergence. Nature does not calculate work or effort; she allows each fork to take care of itself and the blood goes where the fork allows. The reasons that forks occur in the first place may be various — because of obstructions, abrasion of cell walls, electrical dissociations, and so on — but again, those are specific forces acting at specific locations without regard for overall plan. Nature does not premeditate; she does not use mathematics; she does not deliberately produce whole patterns, she lets whole patterns produce themselves. Nature does what nature demands; she is beyond blame and responsibility.

Modular Trees

WITH RANDOM NUMBERS and calculations of least effort we have generated some patterns that look like real trees. Real trees, however, do not grow in a random or irregular fashion like a random network. Real trees generate their parts in a regular and uncompromising manner and only end up looking random after disease and competitive struggle have taken their toll. Trees grow in a repetitive or modular manner. In any particular species, every bud is like every other bud and at the time of its propagation every bud is related to its neighbors in the same way. We will see specific examples of the growth of trees in the next chapter. Here, however, let us investigate some general patterns of repetitive growth.

If we start with a unit, say the largest "Y" in Figure 98a which has a branching angle of 75°, and we add similar but smaller units to the tip of each branch, and then add to the branches of those units similar but still smaller units, continuing the additive process three times, we will use the four types of units in frame a to generate the tree in frame b. (The stems of the units are dotted to indicate that when they join the next larger unit they overlap its branches.) A "Horton analysis" of the tree in frame b reveals a bifurcation ratio of exactly 2, the first-order branches being twice as numerous as the second-order branches. That bifurcation ratio follows, of course, from the way the tree is

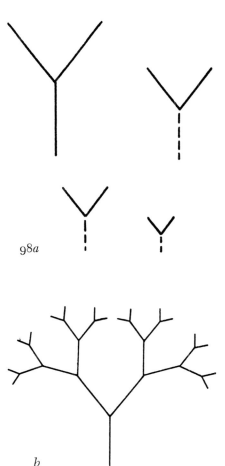

98a

b

generated, each unit in frame *a* being twice as numerous as its predecessor.

In a similar fashion, using the asymmetrical units of Figure 99*a*) we can generate the tree of frame *b* with a bifurcation ratio of exactly 3. At first glance, the regularity of that tree is not apparent, but a little study reveals that analogous parts of analogous branches fork in an identical fashion.

Proceeding as before, we can generate from the units displayed in Figure 100*a* the tree of frame *b* with a bifurcation ratio of exactly 4. Despite the appearance of irregularity, a strict repetition of parts occurs within the pattern.

Now, instead of adding smaller and smaller units, let us keep them all the same size but add units that have both long and short branches. Figure 101*a* shows two "Y's" with unequal branches — the longer branch having twice the length of the shorter. Let us start with the left-hand unit and add to its short branch a unit like itself, while to its long branch let us add a unit similar to the right-hand unit. If we continue adding units in that manner for four generations, we will obtain the tree of frame *b*.

That tree contains only two lengths of line. All lines are drawn with equal thickness. All forks have equal angles. All forks have both a long and a short branch, with the long branch growing to the right from a long limb, and to the left from a short limb. If you travel directly from the root to the extreme tip of any branch you will always encounter four forks. In short, no arbitrary growth occurs. And although simple rules are rigidly followed, note how pleasing and graceful is the overall shape. The tree grows from the regular combination of a module with its mirror image, but appears neither so regular that it is dull nor so irregular that it is completely amorphous. It falls in the narrow range between order and diversity that we find beautiful.

The tree of Figure 101 has a bifurcation ratio of exactly 2; yet it appears far more attractive and natural than the symmetrical tree of Figure 98, which has precisely the same bifurcation ratio and precisely the same number of forks. Can we describe the difference

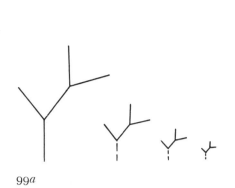

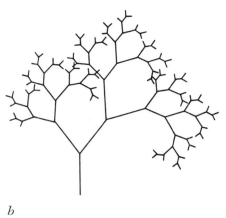

99*a* b

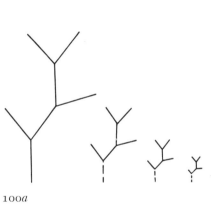

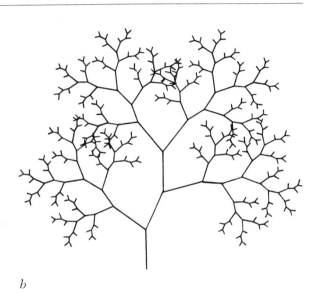

100*a* b

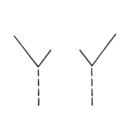

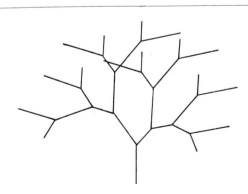

101*a* b

between the two trees quantitatively? Some of the difference undoubtedly lies in the lengths of the branches, but the rest must lie in their arrangement.

Figure 102*a* shows the tree of Figure 98 with lines or "growth contours" that connect centers of branches of equal length. The number on each contour indicates how many branches it connects. Since each branch splits into two branches that in turn split into two more branches, each growth contour intersects twice as many branches as its predecessor. In other words, the number of branches grows in the geometric progression: 1, 2, 4, 8, 16 . . . The trees of Figures 99 and 100 branch with the same geometric progression.

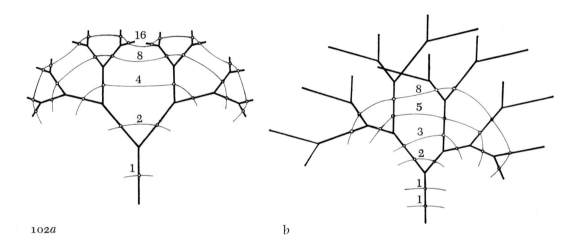

102*a*   b

In Figure 102*b* we see a different progression. Here, if we split long branches into two sections, on the assumption that they take twice as long to grow as short branches, contours of equal growth connect branches according to the progression 1, 1, 2, 3, 5, 8 . . . That number series, in which each term is the sum of the two preceding terms, constitutes the famous Fibonacci series, and, as the progression continues, the ratio between any term and its successor approaches the ratio of the golden section, 1 to 1.61803 . . . (The ratio is noteworthy or "golden" because two dimensions in that ratio bear the unique relation to one another that the smaller is to the larger as the larger is to the sum of them both.)

The Fibonacci series has long served to describe patterns of branching and we shall meet it again in still other contexts. We should note, however, that the series is only one of many number sequences that might be used to describe branching. The tree of Figure 100 whose branches follow a regular geometric progression is as convincing a description of a natural tree as Figure 102*b* based on the Fibonacci progression. The two progressions simply describe different "species" of tree.

Although some of our modular trees look superficially like real trees, their branches overlap, and so they do not look like rivers. We can accept overlapping in two-dimensional portrayals of three-dimensional trees since we can imagine one branch passing in front of another. In a river basin, however, competition between branches occurs in the same plane, and one branch eliminates the other by capturing all its water.

Our modular trees lack another mark of competitive struggle. They exhibit no false starts, no suckers, no branches that start off from the trunk and go nowhere. In contrast, the patterns generated by random numbers grow competitively. As we have seen, some branches lengthen and ramify and others do not, depending upon other branches nearby.

Perhaps we can introduce competition and still generate artificial trees according to simple rules. To that end let us borrow from the work of the mathematician Stanislaw Ulam.

Trees from Rules

Ulam has generated patterns of growth by filling or coloring cells within a regular mosaic according to strict rules. Similar to his patterns is that of Figures 103 and 104, made by coloring successive generations of triangles within a continuous triangular array. The

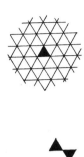

103

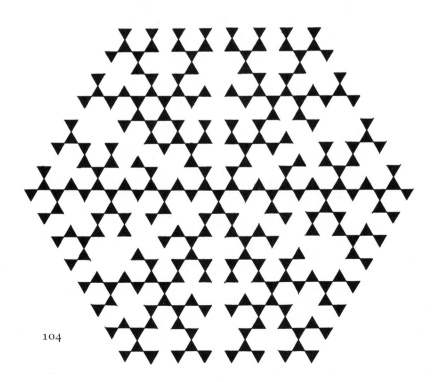

104

105

106

107

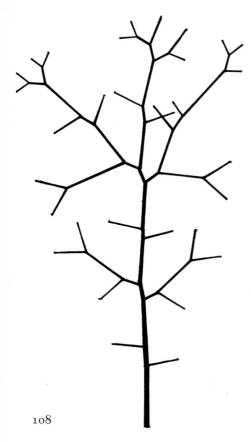

108

rule used is to start with a single triangle and color all subsequent triangles that touch one and only one vertex of a triangle of a preceding generation. Figure 103 shows the first five generations built up one after the other in accordance with the rule. (The guiding triangular grid is omitted after the third generation.)

Figure 104 shows the pattern obtained after fifteen generations and Figure 105 shows the pattern made by linearly connecting the centers of those fifteen generations of triangles.

Figure 105 reveals some interesting regularities. Like a snowflake, the pattern contains six arms. Looking closer, however, we see that the entire pattern is built from a repetition of only one arm that alternates with its mirror image. Figure 106 shows two adjacent arms and we observe that a mirror placed along the dotted line would indeed reflect one arm into the other.

Figure 107 shows one of the six arms after twenty-eight generations. It contains a definite central trunk, but its orderliness and the simplicity of the rule that gives it birth are not at all obvious.

Like rivers and the patterns generated by random numbers, the tree of Figure 107 has bifurcation ratios between three and five, and its highest-order branches are longer than the others. We also see the telltales of competitive struggle that we missed in the modular trees — the branches that do not bear fruit, that end before they have hardly begun. Statistically then, and visually too, the tree of Figure 107 generated by a strict rule is similar to those generated by random numbers, and we observe that profoundly different models can portray the same phenomena equally well. Randomness can appear regular and regularity random.

When we use Murray's graph to determine branching angles of the tree in Figure 107, we obtain the handsome tree of Figure 108. The pattern is similar to Figure 107 in that it has the same number of lines meeting at the same number of junctions. The organic and lifelike appearance of the tree comes about by changing only the angles and widths of the branches.

Note again how the tree of Figure 108 with its over-

lapping branches looks more like a tree than a river —
in contrast to Figure 107. Ideally, of course, we would
like to set the branches of Figure 107 at angles appropriate to describe a river and still obtain a pattern
whose tributaries do not overlap, but Murray's model
for determining angles is independent of Ulam's model
of generating branching, and we cannot use the two
together.

At this point we have explored a variety of methods
to generate branching patterns. Whether random or in
obedience to strict rules, most of the patterns look
superficially like real trees. Most of them have many
little branches affixed to a small number of big ones.
Most of them fan out in space with the bifurcation
ratios that are found in a wide variety of natural phenomena. Let us see now how nature, blind and without mathematical forethought, actually makes a tree.

6

Trees

We must study phyllotaxis which is the bugbear of botany, so simple, yet so profound as to be incomprehensible.

— E. J. CORNER

I**N ACCORD** with Robert E. Horton's observation, we might expect a tree to spread in space so that branches of any given order are three to five times as numerous as branches of the next higher order. Thus, in the typical case, we might expect a tree to look like the lichtenberg figures shown in Figure 91. Although natural trees look superficially like those patterns, they differ in at least one respect: branches of lichtenberg figures uniformly connect interior as well as exterior points, whereas branches of trees, in seeking dense coverage around the periphery in order to soak up sunlight, make contact with relatively few interior points. In the shady interior of the tree, the small branches die, twigs and new leaves fail to develop, and the trunk and major limbs remain smooth and bare.

If we think of the tree as a transportation network for food and water, as a three-dimensional pattern of flow, we would expect it to respect Murray's laws of least work, so that small branches would stick out at right angles from big ones and big branches would stick out at smaller angles from each other. That seems to be the case. Even though the tree is not a hollow conduit like an artery, even though a good deal of it is "solid" structure infiltrated with small and widely dispersed channels, Murray's observations hold. Actually, in view of the pronounced differences between arteries and trees, we should be surprised that the two systems look so much alike.

The Plumbing of Trees

MOST TREES have two transportation networks, one for water, called the xylem, and one for food, called the phloem. Both systems occasionally work under positive pressure, with the roots acting as a pump. It is the root pressure that allows us to tap the xylem of the sugar maple in order to make syrup, much as the aphid taps the phloem of the linden tree. More often, however, the water flows upward under negative pressure: it is pulled rather than pushed.

The pull comes from evaporation in the topmost leaves which drags the water up the tree like a long chain. We can readily determine that the water is not sucked up under a vacuum since water under a vacuum can rise only thirty-three feet, whereas water in a tree often rises ten times as high. In order to be dragged like a chain, the water column must be continuous. No bubbles, air spaces, or partitions can be allowed to interrupt the flow. Winter freezing inevitably causes bubbles to form in the xylem conduits and those bubbles must be absorbed or new conduits grown before flow can start again in the spring. Cell walls can also block the flow of water; consequently the cells of the conduit must die and the intermediate walls dissolve before a continuous channel is formed. The conduit must also be strengthened with lignin, and

the resulting structure, comparable to reinforced concrete, prevents collapse of the cells when the water is pulled through them. Thus the xylem serves a dual function: it not only conducts water but also provides the plant with structural rigidity. It is as though the plumbing system of a house were used as its structural framework as well.

— Zimmermann

The plumbing system, when complete, holds a large volume of water. You can, according to the botanist E. J. Corner, obtain about a quart of "cool, clear, if somewhat earthy-tasting" water from only a ten-foot section of rattan vine.

To a very real extent, the overall shape of the tree is determined by its system of conduits, just as, on a smaller scale, the shape of the leaf is determined by its network of interlocking veins — a fact realized by the artist Paul Klee. (See Figure 109.) In Klee's words,

> The plane form that comes into being is dependent on the interlocking lines. And where the power of the line ends, the contour, the limit of the plane form, arises.

Corner makes a further observation about the veins of leaves:

> Patterns of veins differ greatly according to the kinds of plant and, if they were properly understood and could be described accurately, they would be found as characteristic of plant species as fingerprints of human beings.

If Corner's statement is correct, we might be able to

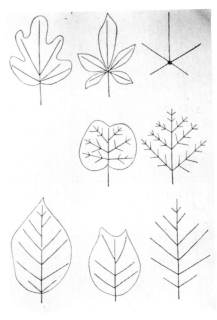

109

110

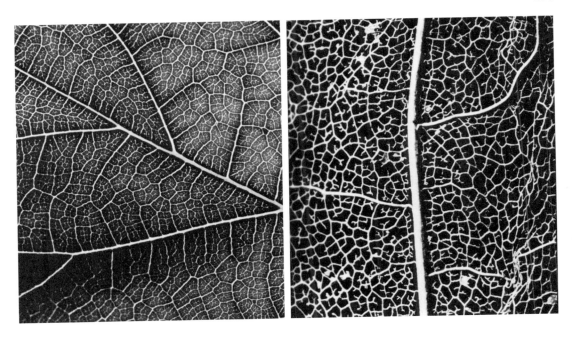

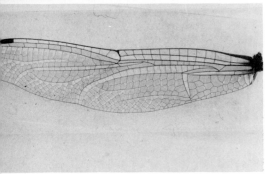

b

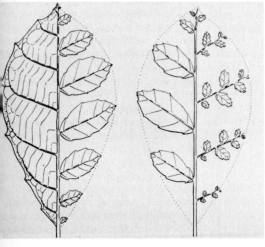

112

perform a "Horton analysis" of the venous network of leaves and derive a statistical system of leaf identification. We might even automate the analysis of veins by means of computer scanning techniques and, through statistical correlation, trace the evolution of leaves in considerable detail.

But again we should remember the differences between veins of leaves and networks of rivers. Leaf veins divide the leaf into separate areas or cells — not microscopic independently nucleated cells, but macroscopic independently irrigated cells. Those cells show clearly in Figure 110. The river system does not form closed cells, nor do rivers flow outward away from the center of the drainage area to form a peripheral vein like the vein in the leaf of Figure 111*a*, or, to jump to the animal world, in the wing of the dragonfly of Figure 111*b*.

Evolution of Trees

THE IRRIGATION SYSTEM of a tree differs in an even more fundamental way from a stream network or a lichtenberg figure. The tree inherits its branching pattern. The tree does not flow automatically from a higher to a lower elevation. By making use of the genetic information contained in the seed, it grows upward against the pull of gravity. If that information is not appropriate to a particular environment, the seed does not sprout, or its issue withers and dies. If the information is miscoded, the issue fails again, except in those rare cases when the mistake turns out to be an asset and inadvertently ushers in a new species that is stronger and more luxuriant than the one before. The surprising part of the story of evolution is that, despite the difficulty of coding information, despite the trial and error and the hit or miss of selective survival, the branching of the tree still resembles the branching of the river. Trees and rivers have no eyes to see each other's patterns. They blindly evolve in their own darkness; and yet they look strikingly similar.

Branching occurs in all parts of the tree, even though the parts differ greatly in function. The trunk and limbs work as structural columns and beams, the roots make a three-dimensional net in which the smallest veins, the root hairs which are protected by dirt, strike off directly from the roots. The smallest veins at the top of the tree are gathered into protective sheaths or leaves that flatten out so as to expose large surfaces to the sun. Each part, although different from the others, branches so that little pieces are added around the periphery to big ones in the center. That is the one directive that has survived countless evolutionary changes and modifications.

With regard to those modifications, it is interesting to observe that evolution has proceeded simultaneously in two different directions — toward simplicity as well as toward complexity. Thus, unlike the jackass that could not decide which of two equally distant hay-stacks to approach, nature moves effortlessly in two opposite directions. She solidifies small leaves into large clusters in one species of plant and in another species breaks a large cluster into fragments. Her right hand does not know the action of her left, so that when one system is about as good as another, she develops both.

With regard to the consolidation of leaves, we observe in Figure 112 (from Corner, 1964) how the stems of leaflets become the veins of larger leaves and how those leaves in turn web together to form a single undivided blade. Many trees have lobed leaves, such as oak and maple, or better still, sycamore and mulberry. Those leaves display an intermediate stage of leaf condensation in which the primitive leaves are only partially fused. Figure 113, for instance, shows three leaves from the same mulberry tree in different stages of evolutionary consolidation.

Although such consolidation simplifies the outline of the leaf, it complicates the veins, for the veins mirror the original branching of the primitive leaflets. The

114a

c

115*a*   *b*

veins, then, record the history of the leaf's evolution.
Note the variety of evolutionary histories revealed by
the simple veins of the Sea Grape, *Coccoloba uvifera*,
of Figure 114*a*, the three major veins in the *Miconia
magnifica* of frame *b*, the complex venous networks of
the *Alcocasia watsoniana* in frame *c*, and the leaf of
the begonia in frame *d*. (The first three photographs
were taken at the Fairchild Tropical Gardens in
Miami, Florida.)

On the other side of the ledger, a single large leaf
may break up into a multitude of small ones. The advantages of small leaves are obvious: they form a
closer mosaic than large leaves, are less easily dam-
aged, and are more easily replaced. Figure 115*a* shows
a large philodendron leaf in the process of breaking up
into small units. The simplicity of the veins tells us
that the leaf is fragmenting rather than consolidating
like the mulberry leaf. The leaf of the philodendron

may be evolving into a mosaic of small leaves like those of the beech, the willow, or the brittle maidenhair (*Adiantum tenerum*) of frame *b* (photographed at Fairchild Tropical Gardens).

Another benefit of small leaves is that they enable the tree to adopt different patterns of growth in different environments. The giant fronds of the palm grow with a strict spiraling symmetry, the same on the north side as on the south, the same to windward as to leeward. Compare the palms of Figure 121 below, which have a strict geometrical leaf development, with the small leaves that the elm puts forth from freely flowing branches like those pictured in Figure 116. The elm fills each chink of its environment with a specially tailored structure, while the palm builds the same edifice for every occasion.

Meristems

OBVIOUSLY EITHER TREND, the consolidation of leaves or their multiplication, is a modification of leaves that already exist. The tree does not suddenly decide to make a large leaf or a number of small leaves where none have lived; it can only modify an existing arrangement.

The most important parts of a growing tree, the parts that must be acted upon if change in form is to arise, are the buds or meristems. The tree cannot put out new growth at any point it chooses, it can grow only at meristems that have been specially prepared in advance. Meristematic growth, growth at only a few points, has developed in trees because new tissue is so delicate that it cannot support itself physically; it must be supported by tough parts that have already grown. And those tough parts cannot themselves reproduce. Specialization in the tree has thus taken place much like specialization in the beehive; the reproductive meristem, like the queen bee, is supported by special-

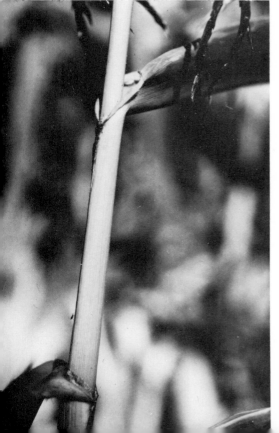

ized offspring that have themselves relinquished the power of reproduction.

A similar specialization occurred in the ink spots discussed in Chapter 4. There growth took place primarily at the tips of the spikes, with surface tension holding the rest of the spot together so as to prevent new areas of growth from getting started. Many plants exhibit similar apical growth in which cell division takes place only at the tips or apexes of the branches. However, in contrast to the spikes of the splash which inhibit indirectly the growth of neighboring parts, the apical meristem produces hormones that inhibit directly the growth of other parts. Thus if an apical bud is removed, areas slightly lower on the stem that are no longer inhibited put forth new buds, whereas, if the apical bud remains intact, lower areas remain dormant.

In the palms, a strange development takes place in the apical meristem. Instead of growing the way fire spreads, by the steady advance of its most forward parts, the leaf grows the way toothpaste squirts from the tube, by being pushed from the bottom. Consequently, the apical meristem becomes a basal meristem. Growth from the base has come to characterize all the palms and their derivatives, with grass and corn, lilies and onions, and hyacinth and crocuses all growing from the bottom and wrapping their sensitive basal meristems in protective sheaths of thick leaves. (See Figures 117 and 51.) With basal growth, of course, you can cut off the top or apex and not destroy the plant. Thus, you can mow the grass or clip your hair with the assurance that it will not die or put out branches.

In addition to pushing the leaf out from the growing point, the basal meristem of the palm extends the trunk above the ground. In a sense, then, it generates new growth in two directions, just as squeezing the center of the tube squirts toothpaste in two directions. An extraordinary double-ended meristem is found in the giant kelp, which grows hundreds of feet in two directions out of a single joint between the stem and the frond.

Another refinement of the meristem occurs in the cambium of a tree, the green layer of new growth just under the bark. The cambium allows living cells distributed around the circumference of the trunk to divide indefinitely (or at least for some forty-six hundred years in the case of the bristlecone pine of California) and it allows the interior tissues of the trunk to harden and support a lofty crown. The tree without a cambium layer, with a soft homogeneous trunk like the palm, supports a less developed crown.

The Xanthorrhoea tree of Australia takes an opposite tack. It keeps its delicate growing parts on the inside of the trunk and pushes sap to the outside where it solidifies to form a solid self-supporting stalk. Whether growing points are on the inside, the outside, at the tips of branches, or at the base, they have become specialized, as in fact have all the parts of the tree. Each part has adapted to its specific task.

The specialization of meristems produces a specialization and limitation of the possible patterns of growth. A tree cannot adopt with equal probability each one of Shreve's distinctly different networks. A tree is confined to the pattern that the distribution of its growing points dictates, and, even more inhibiting, it is confined to the pattern that the individual meristem is able to produce. The meristems are circumscribed, not only in their spatial arrangement but, more especially, in the varieties of growth they can put forth.

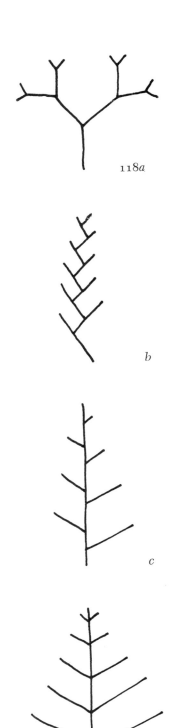

118a

b

c

d

Basic Patterns of Growth

THE MOST PRIMITIVE PATTERN of growth in plants is illustrated in Figures 118a and 98. It is called dichotomous branching: in it the apical meristem of each branch puts out two equal branches, each of which then splits into two more branches. A few plants still branch in the dichotomous manner, chief among them the common club mosses and some of the seaweeds. It has been suggested that all the palms descended from a dichotomous ancestor, although today only the

Hyphaene palms show the true dichotomous habit.

If the doubled branches grow unequally, with the growth of one member exceeding that of the other, a zigzag or overtopping pattern results, as shown in Figure 118*b* — a pattern characteristic of the coral bells in Figure 119.

It is easy to imagine the undeveloped stubs of the overtopping pattern growing leaves and dividing further to become true lateral branches set in the so-called alternate arrangement shown in Figure 118*c*. Figure 120 shows leaves of false Solomon's seal, leaflets of the frond of a coconut palm, and fronds of the traveler's palm, all growing up two sides of the stem in alternating steps.

119

120

The next evolutionary step appears to have occurred when the lateral branches took advantage of the third dimension to grow in spiral succession around the stem. Until that time, plants, like our diagrams, were essentially two dimensional.

121*a*   *b*

Palms, probably the oldest of all flowering plants, provide the most dramatic examples of the spiral succession of leaves. Recently a cartoon in a northern city newspaper showed two men stranded on a deserted tropical island, one of whom was sweeping up palm fronds and remarking to his friend, "You know, Carl, I really hate fall." The cartoon would only make sense to a northerner. People familiar with palms know that those trees do not drop their leaves in the fall but, rather, they drop them throughout the year, usually at the rate of one leaf each month. When a new frond breaks out at the top of the spiral column, an old one dies and falls away at the bottom. Thus the crown of the palm always contains the same number of leaves — about thirty on the coconut palm. (See Figure 121*a*.) And since the leaves drop off at monthly intervals, each leaf of the coconut palm is functional for about thirty months. A similar spiral succession and time interval controls the development of the leaf within the bud, so that the total life of the leaf, from inception within the bud until it falls from the tree, is 2×30 months, or about five years.

The sequential growth of fronds makes it possible to

determine the age of a palm tree by adding the age of its fronds to the age of its trunk, the age of the trunk being determined by the number of leaf scars that it bears. The leaf scar of the coconut palm is the crescent-shaped mark that remains on the trunk after the frond falls away. In some palms the scars are actually leaf stalks that protrude like tusks, as, for example, in the *Corypha elata* in Figure 121*b* (photographed at Fairchild Tropical Gardens). Multiplying the number of leaf scars on a palm trunk by the time interval between successive leaves gives the age of the trunk. Then if you add the age of the fronds, plus the amount of time the tree grows before the trunk develops (about five years for the coconut palm), you can determine the total age of the tree. That is the only method you can use to ascertain the age of a palm since its trunk has no annual rings to count. Its xylem and phloem conduits are not confined to a circumferential layer of cambium that alternately grows and rests. The conduits are used continuously and are distributed uniformly through the pulpy stem like the strings in a piece of celery.

E. J. Corner reports still another consequence of the sequential development of palm fronds.

A more complicated deduction enables us to understand the differences in stature among palms. If, for simplicity, all palm-leaves are assumed to grow at the same rate, a big leaf will take longer than a small leaf and it will have a longer working life equal to its growing time. But a big leaf needs a thick stem to support it and a big food supply to develop it. A thick stem in palms means a stout stem-apex and, other things being equal, a stout stem-apex will develop more leaves around it than a small apex. Therefore, palms with stout trunks should have large crowns of many large and long-lived leaves whereas those with slender trunks should have small crowns of few, small, and relatively short-lived leaves. This is exactly what is found. . . .

The spiral habit of phyllotaxis or leaf arrangement

is common to many other plants and trees besides palms and we shall shortly study it in more detail. Out of the spiral or helical pattern of growth, however, comes a quite different pattern, one that develops when the axis of the helix compresses like a spring so that the plant, instead of putting out leaves one after the other, puts out a whorl of leaves or branches that completely encircles the stem. Figure 122 shows the Norfolk Island pine which puts out whorls of branches at successive intervals along its trunk. Whorls may be succeeded by other whorls further up the stem and each whorl may be rotated relative to its neighbors. The petals of flowers make whorls and, interestingly enough, the number of petals in a flower is often one of the terms of the Fibonacci series. For example, there are 3 petals in the iris, 5 in the primrose, 13 in the ragwort, 21 in the marigold, and 34, 55, and 89 in different kinds of daisies.

122

Whorls of two leaves in which the leaves grow directly opposite one another are also common. Those, double-bladed whorls may rotate as they climb the stem as in baby's breath, lantana, and spearmint, or they may lie instead in the same plane as diagrammed in Figure 118d, the pattern of walnut, ash, and sumac. Africa produces a Welwitschia tree that has only one double-leafed whorl. The tree grows to about a foot in height but the trunk can have a three-foot diameter and the two leaves grow continuously for thousands of years, piling up on the ground in a tangled mass like a heap of trash.

The interesting point about those patterns is that they are directly determined by cell division in the meristem. Furthermore, since all the meristems in a given plant are the same, the pattern of growth is the same throughout all parts of the plant. The only variation is whether the pattern of growth will develop fully, whether each bud will produce leaves. The pattern of possibilities is fixed; only the realization varies. Furthermore, since, as Leonardo da Vinci observed, "the branches always start above the leaf," that is, in the fork between the leafstalk and the stem, it is phyllotaxis — or the arrangement of leaves on the stem — that fixes the arrangement of twigs on a branch and, as growth continues, the arrangement of branches on a limb. Phyllotaxis also determines the shapes of the flowers and even the arrangement of the reproductive parts within the flowers.

Take the lilac for example.

Frame a of Figure 123 shows a cross section through the bud of the lilac and we see the compressed young leaves stacked in pairs that are set at right angles to one another. Frames b and c show typical pairs of vegetative and floral branches, and frame c shows a less typical mixed pair in which one branch has developed leaves and the other has developed flowers. In that frame we can see that the crossed or decussate arrangement first visible in the bud is maintained by both the leaves and the groups of flower buds, that is to say, both the leaves and buds are set on the stem in pairs so that each pair crosses at right angles the pair immediately above and below. The leaves thus grow on the stem in the same way that they pack in the bud. The only change is an elongation of the stem. In frame e we see that the flower is a modification of the same plan. The two pairs of petals unite to form a four-lobed flower. When one of the petals is removed, as in the last frame, we can see that the two stamens which carry pollen are attached directly to one pair of petals, while below and aligned at right angles to them sits the double-lobed stigma to which the pollen adheres. Thus the buds, leaves, branches, petals, and reproductive parts of the flower are variations on the same decussate arrangement.

It is that structural consistency in organic forms that so impressed Frank Lloyd Wright.

Along the wayside some blossom, with unusually glowing color or prettiness of form attracts us; we accept gratefully its perfect loveliness; but, seeking to discover the secret of its charm, we find the blossom, whose more obvious claim first arrests our attention, intimately related to the texture and shape of its foliage; we discover a strange sympathy between the form of the flower and the sys-

tem upon which the leaves are arranged about the stalk. From this we are led to observe a characteristic habit of growth, and resultant nature of structure. . . .

Another architect, Le Corbusier, whose sketch is reproduced in Figure 124, was similarly impressed with the consistency of growth in plants and trees.

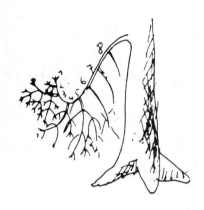

I am in the mountains, drawing an old fir tree that stands in the pasture. I discover a law. "Look," I say to my master, "you can tell the age of the tree from its oldest branch." Here are the three growths of the year, each with its three buds; (a) will provide next year's growth; (b) and (c) will angle off, each in turn yielding three growths with three buds apiece. The law is enunciated. The oldest branch, the one closest to the ground, almost surely initiates a series of growths.

And the entire tree is a pure mathematical function. (This is not an assertion of fact; I have never had the opportunity to prove it.)

If the tree always branches the same way, how regular is its overall shape? Is it true, as Le Corbusier suspected, that the tree is a mathematical function? For an answer, let us look at another example of growth, the maple tree, which has the same decussate pattern of branching found in the lilac.

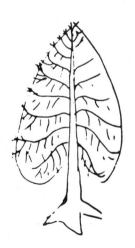

Figure 125a shows the typical pair of flowers at the end of the divided branch. Frames b and c illustrate the decussate arrangement of leaf stems in which each pair sits at right angles to the pair immediately above and below. Frame d shows a typical pair of pistils and frame e a close-up of one of the pistils which is composed of two winged seeds surmounted by a divided stigma. Like the lilac then, the parts of the maple come in pairs and the pairs grow at right angles to one another.

The last two frames of Figure 125 show the trunk and branches of mature maple trees. Where is the decussate arrangement? Where is the structural consistency? The tree in frame g has an overall order to it,

25a

b

c

d

e

f

g

but, rather than forming regular repetitive pairs, the branches flow like lines in a lichtenberg figure. How did the decussate pattern become random?

Incredible as it may seem, every branch in the tree grew out of a fork between a stem and a leafstalk, and every leaf was opposed by another leaf or a bud that could generate leaves. At the time of their inception, all the buds held primitive leaves in the decussate arrangement. The randomness came about because some of the buds received no light or were broken off so they did not elongate into stems, or, if they did develop, the stems twisted and turned in response to sun, shade, wind, and snow. Consequently, the reason the mature maple looks random is because some of its parts did not develop fully or developed in a twisted or misshapen manner.

126*a*

b

The branches of the forsythia in Figure 126 provide a clear example of how sunlight modifies the inherited pattern of decussate branching. In frame *a* we see pairs of shoots working their way up the stem with each pair crossing adjacent pairs at right angles. Frame *b* shows a bifurcated branch from the same bush, but one that grows horizontally instead of vertically. On the horizontal branch only the buds at the top which are exposed to sunlight develop shoots. If buds on the lower side of the branch develop, they twist around until they also face upward. Thus all the shoots stick straight up.

Thinking about the decussate pattern for a moment, we realize how fortunate it is that the pattern can be modified. The pattern, if rigidly adhered to, would inevitably lead to conflict. Leaves and branches would grow into one another. We see the beginnings of that conflict in frame c of Figure 125 where the lower leaf-stalks of the maple have put forth additional pairs of leaves that would hit the stalks of the leaves above if one or the other pairs did not twist out of the way. As a theoretical model then, the decussate pattern is not a good configuration for branching. It contains inherent conflicts and works only because it can be modified. Thus, to the extent that he did not consider environmental modifications, Le Corbusier missed the mark with his hypothesis: as well as being a pure mathematical function, the tree responds directly to its environment.

Spiral Phyllotaxis

IN REVIEWING different types of phyllotaxis or leaf arrangements, we learned that the alternate pattern of branching depicted in Figure 118c, in which the leaves grow on opposite sides of the stem but at different heights, may have evolved into the spiral or helical pattern, in which the leaves circle around the stem. Evolution may have moved in the opposite direction as well, that is to say, the helical pattern may have produced the alternate pattern. In any case, let us look now at the meristem of the helical pattern, for the pattern grows in accord with terms of the Fibonacci series and has therefore aroused lively interest.

Figure 127 shows a cross section of a bunch of celery just above its meristem (the conical mound of solid tissue at the base of the plant), and we see how the stalks pack together and overlap one another in a

127

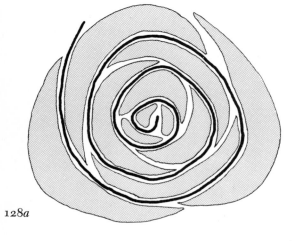

128a

b

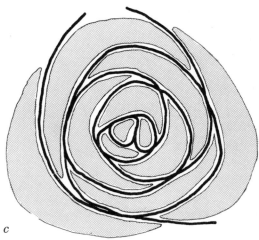

c

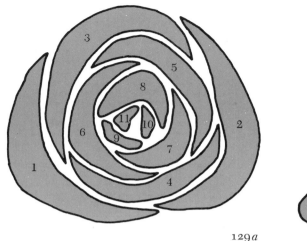
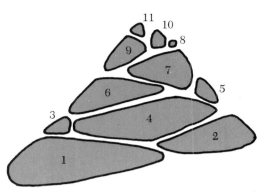

129a   b

swirling pattern. As analyzed in Figure 128, a single counterclockwise spiral (*a*) and a double spiral (*b*) are superimposed (*c*) to outline the stalks of the celery. In the figure, the spirals fall between the stalks, but they could as well run through the centers of the stalks. In either case, we would find one spiral superimposed upon two.

Figure 129 is a diagram of the celery with the stalks labeled in the order in which they develop. Frame *b* of the figure shows how the stalks join the meristem in oval attachments, rather like the leafstalks of the philodendron shown in Figure 50. In both examples, the stalks spiral up the stem, except that in the celery the stem is a flat cone rather than a long cylinder.

The helical pattern arises because the leaves develop one at a time — in contrast to the opposite and decussate patterns where they develop two at a time — and each leaf grows in the largest available gap between existing leaves. Checking the plan view of the celery stalks, we see that stalk 3 fits in the gap between stalks 1 and 2, stalk 5 fits between stalks 2 and 3, stalk 8 between stalks 5 and 6, etc., so that each new stalk grows where it has the most room.

A less obvious observation, but one that is borne out again by the photograph and the figure is that, in nesting against a pair of stalks, the new stalk rides over the older of the pair so that, in plan view, its

130

center is closer to the center of the older rather than the younger stalk. In the top of Figure 129, for instance, we see that stalk 3 is closer to stalk 1 than to stalk 2, stalk 6 is closer to stalk 4 than stalk 3, and so forth. That positioning happens automatically; the older of the pair of stalks sits lower on the stem so that the new stalk rides over it.

Now, depending on the size of the leaf bases and how fast they diminish in size as they climb the cone of the meristem, different variations of the helix come into existence. We can see that if the leaves diminish rapidly in size, stalk 4 starts lower in the gap between stalks 1 and 2 and leaves room at the sides between stalks 3 and 5 for stalks 6 and 7. In that event, the whorls of the spiral compress so that the stalks in one whorl squeeze through the gaps between the stalks in the preceding whorl to contact stalks of a still earlier whorl. If the leaf bases diminish at a still faster rate, the whorls compress further so that the leaf bases of one whorl touch those two, three, or four whorls away. In a real sense, those compressed patterns of helical growth are only variations on the basic pattern of Figure 129. In any of the more compressed forms, for example, stalk 6 sits between stalks 3 and 4 just as in our diagram, but stalks 3 and 4 are small enough to allow stalk 6 to sneak between them and make contact with stalk 1. Whether or not the stalks in one whorl interpenetrate the stalks in another, they always grow in each other's gaps, so that, except for displacements that arise from compression of the whorls, they keep the same position relative to one another.

We have thus discovered two important facts about spiral phyllotaxis: (1), when leaf bases develop in succession around the stem apex, they fit between each other so as to align themselves in a helical pattern in which each new stalk rides above the older member of a pair of stalks in the preceding whorl; (2), variations of the helical pattern can develop in which stalks of one whorl interpenetrate and make contact with stalks in previous whorls. Let us see how natural examples fit those facts.

Figure 130 shows the helix of thorns that develops

on a young hawthorn tree. If you spiral upwards, passing twice around the stem, you pass through five thorns and come to a thorn almost directly above the one at which you started. That particular phyllotaxis is commonly represented by the fraction $\frac{2}{5}$, the numerator describing the number of times you circle the stem and the denominator describing the number of leaves, branches, or thorns you pass through. Apple, oak, and apricot have the same $\frac{2}{5}$ pattern of phyllotaxis; sedges, beech, and hazel have a phyllotaxis of $\frac{1}{3}$; plantain, poplar, and pear have a phyllotaxis of $\frac{3}{8}$; and leeks, willow, and almond have a phyllotaxis of $\frac{5}{13}$. The numerators and denominators of those fractions are terms in the Fibonacci series: 1, 2, 3, 5, 8, 13, ... Although examination of the meristems reveal that the designated leaves or branches do not line up exactly with one another, they come close enough for the Fibonacci fractions to prove useful in the description of growth patterns in plants and trees.

The Fibonacci numbers occur in an even more dramatic and precise manner in the compound spirals of Figure 131. In those examples, the numerator and denominator of the fraction give the number of clockwise and counterclockwise spirals. Accordingly, the celery of Figure 127 has a phyllotaxis of $\frac{1}{2}$ and the pineapple of Figure 131a, as well as the pinecone shown in Figure 131b, both of which have 8 rows of florets or scales spiraling one way and 13 spiraling the other, have a phyllotaxis of $\frac{8}{13}$. Other species of pinecone have a phyllotaxis of $\frac{2}{3}$, $\frac{3}{5}$, or $\frac{5}{8}$. The daisy of frame c has a phyllotaxis of $\frac{21}{34}$, exactly the same as the sunflower of frame d, although $\frac{55}{89}$ and $\frac{89}{144}$ are also common in sunflowers, and Daniel T. O'Connell reports growing a granddaddy sunflower with a phyllotaxis of $\frac{144}{233}$.

The reason that all those fractions are made from successive terms of the Fibonacci series is that they are all variations of the same helical pattern of growth; they are all variations on the celery.

In order to prove the point, let us consider a diagram that shows the distribution of celery stalks. It will also show the distribution of florets in pinecones,

b

c

d

daisies, and sunflowers. That is to say, one diagram will depict all the Fibonacci fractions.

That diagram is Figure 132a. It is an array of points laid out in succession along the spiral shown in frame b. In a however, the generating spiral is omitted. The points bear a special relation to one another as you can ascertain by drawing a line that connects any point with the center and observing how it sits relative to the pair of points just beyond it. Assuming that the points grow from the periphery of the spiral inward toward the center, you find in every case that the line through the chosen point makes less of an angle with the "older" of the two distant points, that is to say, it falls closer to the point laid down earlier than to the point laid down later. That relation is just what we observed in the celery stalks. In plan view, the line through the center of each stalk makes a small angle with the center of the older stalk and a large angle with the center of the younger stalk.

The points of Figure 132a are laid out along the spiral in b so that the circular arc between any two consecutive points is 137.5°, or, to be more precise, 137° 30′ 28″. Why that special angle? Because it has something to do with plant tissues? No. The angle only sets the points in the proper relation to one another, so that each point makes a small angle with the older point in the previous whorl and a large angle with the younger point. That relation comes about quite naturally in the meristem of the plant as a direct result of each stalk's fitting the gaps of other stalks; but to draw the relation in a two-dimensional diagram, we have to use some mathematics. It happens that the special angle of nearly 137.5° is 360° times $(3 - \sqrt{5})/2$ and that in terms of the golden section, ϕ or .618 . . . , it is 360° times ϕ^2. In terms of the Fibonacci series it approximates 360° times one term in the series divided by the term directly after the next succeeding one. Thus the angle has a definite meaning in terms of the golden section and the Fibonacci series, but, of course, the growing plant does not care about such matters. The plant uses no mathematics, it simply grows the stalks where they have the most room; we

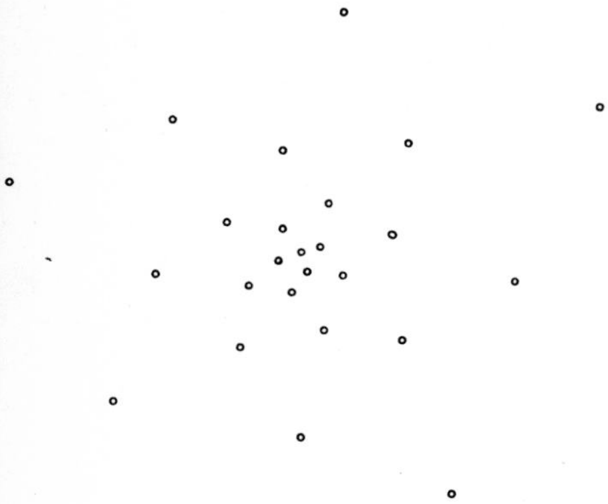

a

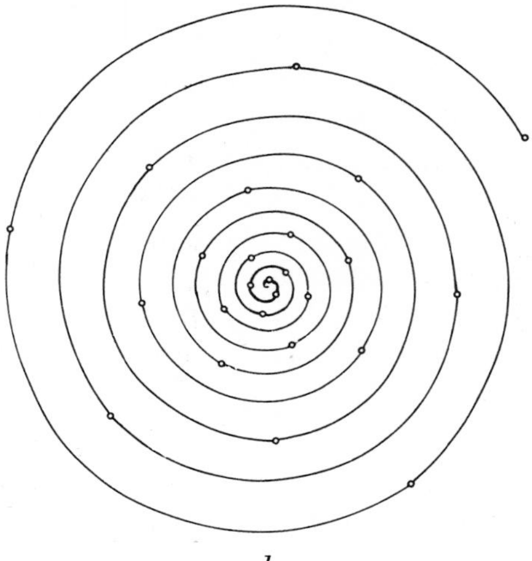

b

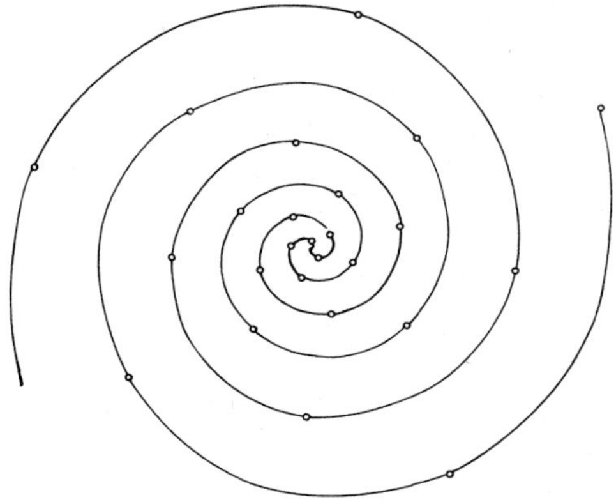

c

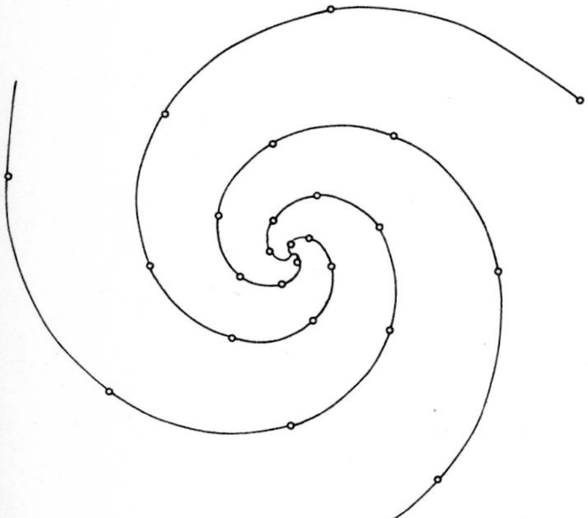

d

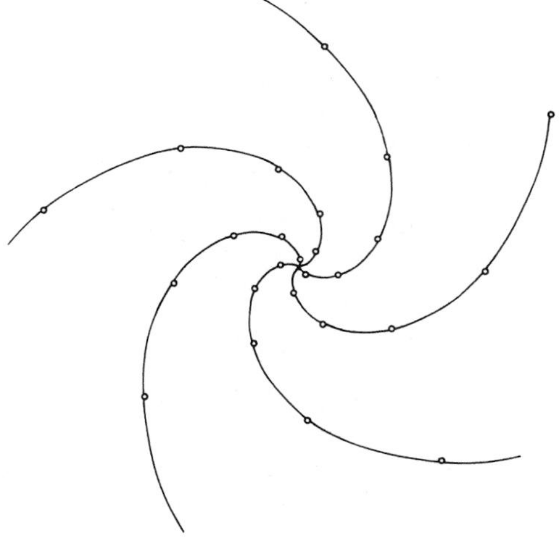

e

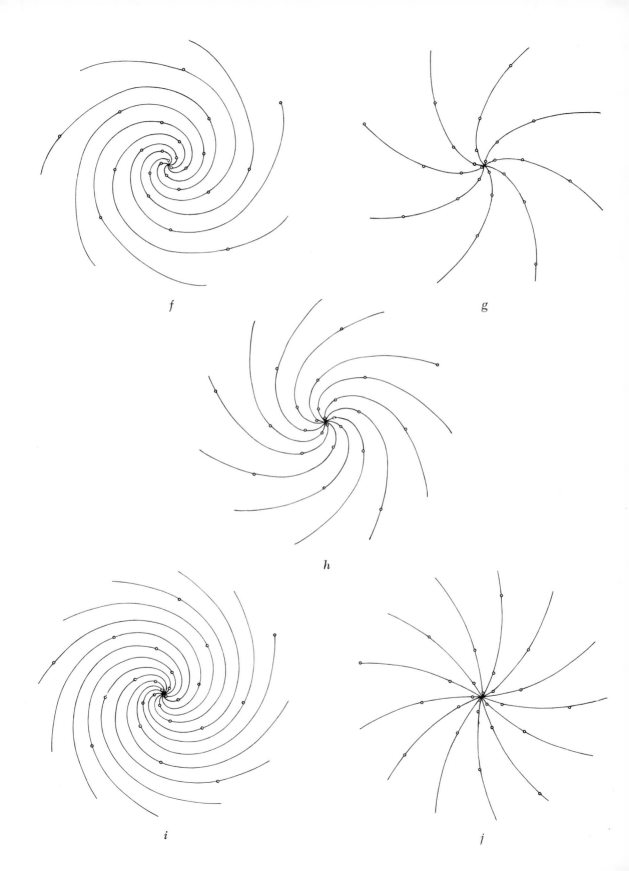

f

g

h

i

j

introduce the mathematics in order to describe the three-dimensional pattern of growth with a two-dimensional diagram.

After the points are laid out, the other frames in Figure 132 show what we can do with them. All in all, as shown in frames *b* through *j*, we can draw groups of 1, 2, 3, 5, 7, 8, 11, 12, and 13 spirals through them. It is interesting to observe that we cannot draw regular groups of 4, 6, 9, and 10 spirals through the points. They do not fit.

Then, after we have drawn the spirals, Figure 133 shows how we can superimpose them. The single spiral overlaps the double spiral in *a*, just as in the diagram of the celery in Figure 128, the group of 2 spirals overlaps the group of 3 in *b*, the group of 3 fits with the group of 5 in *c*, the 5 work with 8 in *d*, and 8 go with 13 in *e*. Thus, through the same array of points, we have drawn compound spirals with Fibonacci fractions of $\frac{1}{2}$, $\frac{2}{3}$, $\frac{3}{5}$, $\frac{5}{8}$, and $\frac{8}{13}$. We could draw other Fibonacci fractions as well, since we can draw 21 spirals through the array that nicely overlap with the 13, and we can draw 34 spirals that will go with the 21, etc.

Furthermore, and this is quite surprising, if the two groups of spirals that we superimpose spiral in opposite directions, and if they cross only at the points in the original array, we get only Fibonacci fractions. Since we cannot draw certain sets of spirals through the given points, and since some of those that we can draw we cannot superimpose on others because they either spiral the wrong way or overlap the others so as to generate additional points, it turns out that our array not only generates *all* Fibonacci fractions, it generates *only* Fibonacci fractions.

Just as the pattern of compound spirals with a phyllotaxis of $\frac{1}{2}$ in Figure 133*a* looks a good deal like the pattern of the celery, we could modify the pattern of spirals with a phyllotaxis of $\frac{8}{13}$ depicted in Figure 133*e* to look like the pattern of the pinecone of Figure 131*b* simply by compressing the whorls, that is to say, by laying out the original points of the array on a more tightly wound spiral than that of Figure 132*b*.

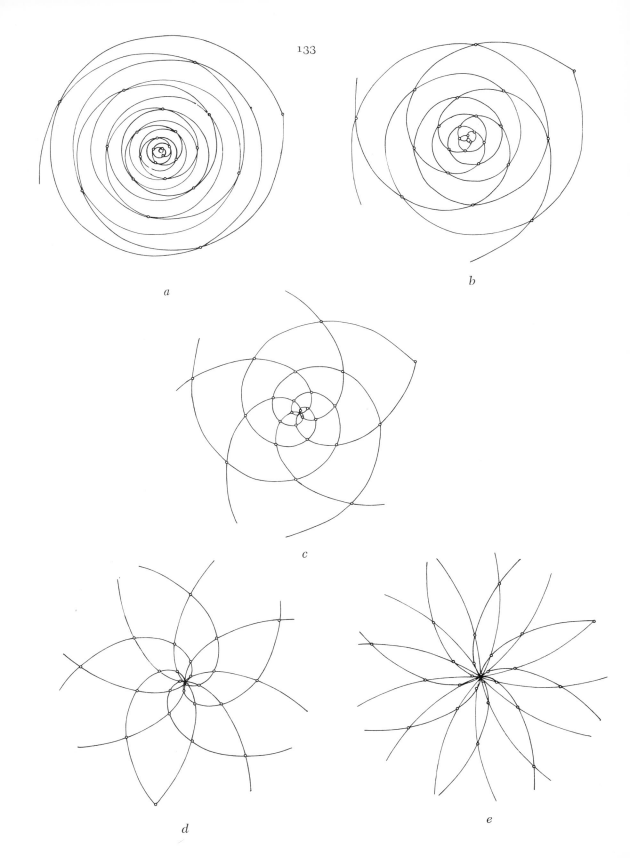

a

b

c

d

e

The important idea is that the points in Figure 132*a* (or some slightly more compressed variation of points), which are generated through the use of the "Fibonacci angle" of 137.5°, mark the intersection of spirals that we find in many growing plants. Although the special angle 137.5° is important to laying out the two-dimensional array of points, and although the relations of that angle to terms in the Fibonacci series give rise to 1, 2, 3, 5, 8, 13, etc., groups of spirals, the plant itself makes no use of the angle or the precision of growth implied by the angle, it simply grows its stalks or florets in succession around the apex of the stem so that each fits the gaps of the others. The plant is not in love with the Fibonacci series; it does not seek beauty through the use of the golden section; it does not even count its stalks; it just puts out stalks where they will have the most room. All the beauty and all the mathematics are the natural by-products of a simple system of growth interacting with its spatial environment.

7

Soap Bubbles

SOAP FILMS ARRANGE THEMSELVES in the minimum network shown earlier in Figure 26, the network characterized by triple junctions and an angle between partitions of 120°. Like other patterns we have investigated, the minimum network exists in a large variety of different systems, but here, in films of soap and water, it manifests its purest form.

Soap Films

THAT SOAP FILMS form minimum surfaces is proved by the simple experiment illustrated in Figure 134, in which a small loop of thread is supported on a soap film stretched across a metal ring. Pricking the film in the center of the loop causes the film around the outside to pull the loop open to make a perfect circle. The hole inside the loop of thread becomes as large as possible, and therefore circular, because the film around the outside becomes as small as possible.

Without disrupting the film, you can easily push the open loop of thread here and there within the metal ring. That pushing and pulling does not change the area of the film outside the loop. But you cannot deform the loop. Any deformation increases the area of the film on the outside. When you force the loop to close, the film automatically pulls it open again.

The soap film holds open the loop just as firemen hold open a net — by pulling outward in all directions.

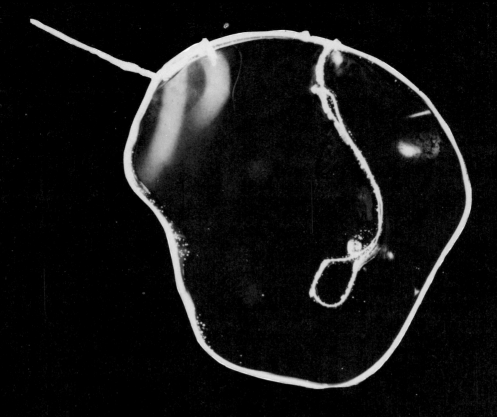

134 *a*

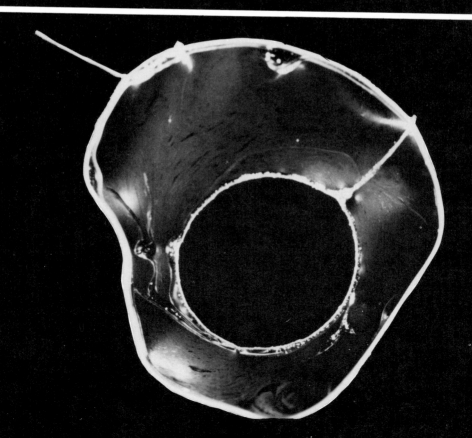

b

Why does the film pull outward? Why does it seek to minimize its area? Because particles of soap and water on the top and bottom surfaces of the film are more strongly attracted to particles of soap and water inside the film than to particles of air outside. The particles seek closer proximity with themselves than with their exterior surroundings. Consequently, on the molecular level, the peaceful film is a scene of frenzied activity. The surface particles are continually getting pulled inside and displacing particles already there, particles which then are themselves pulled inside.

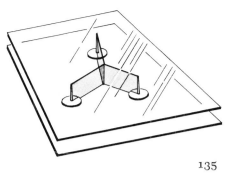

135

Partitions

Now, by means of another demonstration, we can see how the tendency of soap and water to form minimum surfaces produces minimum networks with regular three-way junctions. Figure 135 shows three thumb-tacks sitting points upward between two sheets of glass. When the entire sandwich of glass and thumb-tacks is dipped into a soap solution and then with-drawn, soap films clinging to the tacks join in a three-way corner. The diagram at the top of Figure 136 shows the triple junction: the three dots represent the vertical shanks of the tacks and the three lines meeting at 120° represent cross sections of the three vertical films.

The interesting fact is that, when the three films meet at 120°, they use less material than they would if they came together in any other way. With a little plane geometry, you can easily prove that in the diagram at the top of Figure 136 the films have 58% of the length they would have if they traveled directly from tack to tack around the perimeter, as in the middle diagram, and 87% of the material they would have if they connected the tacks with only two lengths of film, as shown at the bottom. Thus, of the three systems of partitions shown in the figure, the three-way 120° junction uses the least material. In the early nineteenth

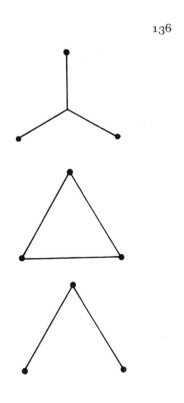

136

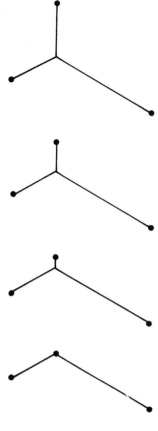

century, Jakob Steiner generalized those results and proved that systems of partitions with three-way corners use less material than any other system.

Let us experiment further with the thumbtack sandwich. In the top diagram of Figure 136 the tacks are arranged at the vertexes of an equiangular triangle, whereas in Figure 137 the tacks sit at the vertexes of triangles with unequal angles. With regard to the formation of the triple junction, we now observe a general rule: the junction moves toward the tack that sits at the vertex commanding the largest angle. Furthermore, as a special case of the rule, we observe that when the triangle outlined by the tacks has a vertex with an angle of 120° or more, the triple junction degenerates and joins the tack that marks that vertex.

Now let us add a fourth thumbtack to the sandwich. If the four tacks sit at the vertexes of a square, we might expect the partition to meet at a central four-way junction, as depicted in the middle diagram of Figure 138. Indeed, that system of partitions uses 94% of the material that would be used to enclose the square on three sides, as shown at the right. However, if we withdraw the four-tack sandwich from the soap solution, the films adopt the still more economical system of partitions pictured in the diagram at the left. That system, with two triple junctions, uses 91% of the

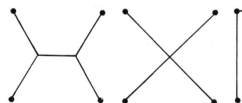

material that would be used to enclose the square on three sides. The double three-way junction and the single four-way junction are thus not very different, representing 91% and 94% of three sides of a square, and yet the soap films unerringly choose the one and not the other.

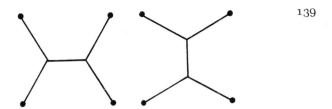

Does the four-way junction ever occur in soap films? Momentarily, yes. By gently blowing through the glass tube of an eyedropper on the central segment of film, you can distort the partitions so that four films come together at a point, but then, when you stop blowing, the films will immediately separate, regrow the central segment, and return to form the original pattern in its original position, or in a position obtained by rotating the original through 90°. Figure 139 shows the pattern in its two positions. One configuration is the other one turned on its side.

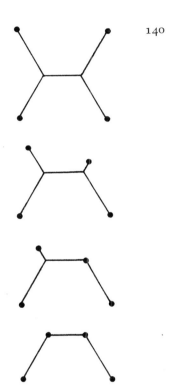

In the same way the triple junction moves toward the largest angle of the triangle, it moves toward the largest angle of the quadrilateral. Figure 140 makes clear the movement and degeneration of the two triple junctions as the four thumbtacks are moved. As with the triangle, the degeneration of a triple junction occurs at a corner with an angle of 120° or more.

Suppose you blow on films that interconnect the vertexes of an irregular quadrilateral like the one shown in Figure 141. You may be able to get them to make a four-way junction, but this time when they separate, they will adopt either of two different con-

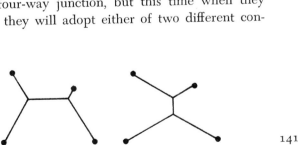

141

figurations. And now you will observe a curious fact. The partition system on the left in Figure 141 is

142

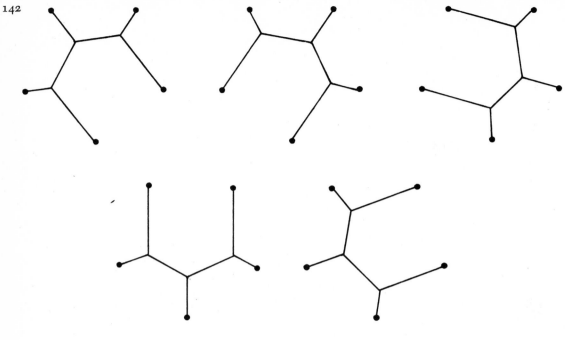

143

shorter than the one on the right. Both configurations are minimum systems of partitions, but one is more minimum than the other! In forming the network of films on the right, the soap particles apparently make a tactical error. They extend themselves more than if they had made the other network.

The tactical error made by the soap particles in choosing a not-so-minimum arrangement is the same sort of error that raindrops make when they fall in the mountains. They all roll downhill, but some get trapped in mountain lakes and some flow into streams that eventually reach the sea. The drop that rolls to the sea reaches a lower altitude or potential energy than the one in the mountain lake, but for the given terrain both find positions of least energy. In exactly the same way, the particles of soap and water move toward a configuration of minimum energy, and, depending on how the thumbtack sandwich is withdrawn from the soap solution, the films may take one configuration or another. Blowing on the films to transform them from one pattern to another is like rolling the raindrop back up the hill. At the top of the hill the drop may well elect to roll down the other side. Similarly, after the films are forced to meet four at a time, they may elect, when they separate, to take up the other configuration.

We have used four tacks in the sandwich. Suppose we add more. A regular arrangement of five tacks gives rise to three triple junctions, and the network of films can adopt any of the five positions shown in Figure 142. Six thumbtacks produce four triple junctions in either of the positions shown in Figure 143, even though those configurations have 4% more length than the configuration that joins five of the tacks directly. Which of the patterns in Figure 143 that gets adopted depends on how you draw the sandwich from the soap solution. Each configuration lies at the lowest point in a separate energy sink, and you can get from one to another only by blowing the junction of films back up the hill.

Suppose we add a whole batch of tacks to our sandwich, say, thirty. We might get a configuration of films

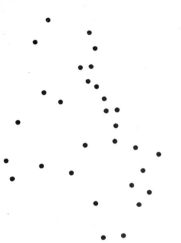

144

like that shown in Figure 144. The topological formula that we have already used several times tells us that we will have 28 triple junctions if none of them degenerate. The formula is

$$J_1 - J_3 = 2$$

that is to say, the number of points (or one-way junctions), less the number of three-way junctions, equals two. We used the formula to describe the branching of rivers in Chapter 5, but observe now how neatly it describes the topological properties of soap films in Figures 136 to 144.

Shrinking Surfaces

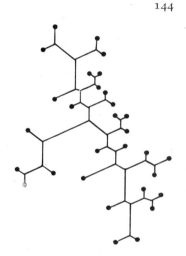

145

SUPPOSE YOU REMOVE all the thumbtacks, press the glass plates together within the soap solution, withdraw them, and then separate them. You will get a pattern like that in Figure 145. Note how that photograph resembles Figure 144, which shows a minimum network of films.

Instead of soap solution between the glass plates, try a drop of poster paint. Figure 146 shows the branching pattern made by the drop of paint after the glass sheets are pulled apart. Again you see a network of interconnected films, but this time the pattern is much more complicated than anything generated with thumbtack sandwiches.

Complications enter because more than a single force is involved. The material flows as well as shrinks. It minimizes work as well as area.

If you pull the plates apart slowly, you will see that the solution flows to the place where the gap between the plates is the narrowest. The solution flows away from where the sheets are the most separated to where they are the least separated. Knowing that, you would be correct to surmise that the sheets must have separated first in the upper right-hand portion of Figure 145 and at the bottom of Figure 146. The material

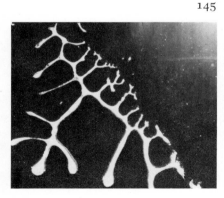

flowed in ever-thickening branches away from those places of initial disengagement.

The process of flow cuts down on the 120° angles that would arise if only surface tension was present. We recall that Murray predicted angles of 75° to represent the minimum separation of two equal branches under conditions of "pure flow," and 120° to represent the separation of equal branches under conditions of "pure surface tension." Accordingly, in a situation in which both flow and surface tension are present, as when we separate two sheets of glass, we would expect to find angles between 75° and 120°. The angles in the poster paint fall within that range.

It is also instructive to look between the glass plates when they are only partially separated. Figure 147*a* shows such a view. You can see the telltale 120° joints. For a more viscous material, like rubber cement, separation of the sheets of glass produces the pattern in frame *b* in which the 120° joints are much modified. We are reminded of the reinforcement between the top and bottom shells of the horseshoe crab in Figure 19*e*. Perhaps that reinforcement arises through the agency of surface tension as the shells separate during growth.

We can easily observe other examples of shrinking surfaces. One in which the three-way junctions are particularly well defined is the scalded milk of Figure 148*a*, where a residue remains in a minimum configuration after the rest of the milk has boiled away. In frames *b* and *c* we see that melting snow on grass and froth on an ocean wave cling to themselves to minimize their surfaces.

Shrinkage of surfaces allows us to understand the dramatic coincidence of form in Figure 149: why the shell of the box turtle looks like a regular cluster of bubbles. We know that the films between the bubbles minimize their area so as to join one another at 120°. The same holds for the lines between the plates of the shell. New cells grow along those lines and gravitate outward to join the edges of the plates. Consequently, as the plates increase in size, the lines between them keep to a minimum.

147*a*

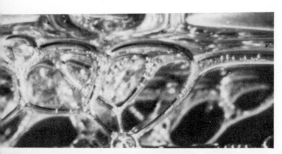

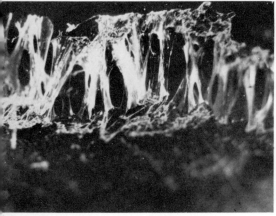

b

149a

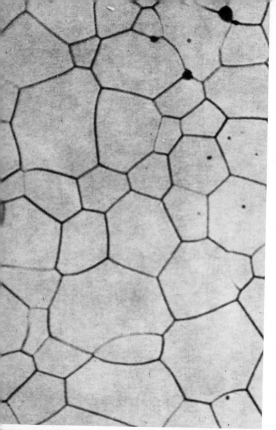

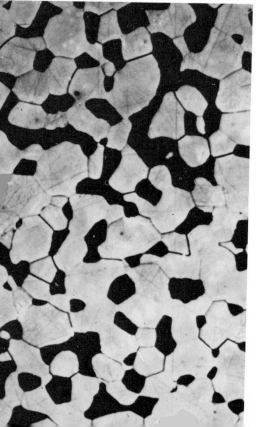

Crystal Grains

WE NOW UNDERSTAND a quite general kind of growth, for it turns out that the deposition of cells to make the plates of a turtle's shell is much like the deposition of atoms and molecules to make the grains of a crystal.

A crystal grain consists of a group of atoms or molecules stacked in orderly rows and layers like grapefruit on a shelf. Each molecule nests comfortably with its neighbors. When other molecules of a similar kind fall into the gaps along the surface of the grain, the grain grows. It continues to grow until it meets another grain. If the two grains have different orientations, a squabble breaks out regarding control of the atoms or molecules in between. Those molecules in the middle do not know which way to turn and they scamper about in a state of excited indecision. However, since the temptation to join with a grain is always present, the number of molecules in the no man's land between the grains is always a minimum. In other words, the boundary between grains is minimized, just like the boundary between the plates of the shell and the boundary between bubbles. And thus it is that the crystal grains in the micrograph of Figure 150 look like bubbles.

Figure 151 shows a crystal with two types of grains. Apparently the surface of the black grains exerts a little more pull or attraction than the surface of the white grains. That extra pull enables the black grains to isolate themselves from the white grains, just as the melting snow isolates itself from the grass and air. Note that the boundaries of the black grains are not much distorted by the boundaries between white grains. The boundaries between white grains join the boundaries of the black grains at less than 120°, whereas they join each other at exactly 120°.

The pattern in Figure 152 also looks like two types of crystal grains. Here, however, the "grains" are the scales of an armadillo. It is not clear whether the scales grow like the plates in the shell of the tortoise or whether they are directly influenced by the effects of

surface tension. It is clear, however, that the interface or boundary between the scales is minimized and only triple junctions occur. And like the black grains in the crystal, the white scales of the armadillo seem to exert a greater pull on those boundaries. The white scales are round and isolated and the boundaries between the black scales join them at less than 120°.

Froth

So FAR we have concerned ourselves primarily with two-dimensional patterns of three-way joints; we have looked at *lines* that make angles of 120°. In actuality, of course, all our patterns are three-dimensional, that is to say, the lines are *partitions* that join one another at 120°.

To see those partitions in their three dimensions, examine the froth of bubbles in the dishpan, in a stein of beer, or on an ocean wave. You see chunks of space, miniature rooms, each one different from its neighbors and yet perfectly interlocked with those neighbors in an incredibly complex three-dimensional jigsaw puzzle.

If you look closely, you see that each line in the froth is the junction of three films that meet one another at 120° and that each line joins three other lines to make a corner that unites six films. Wherever you look, the format is the same: every line is the meeting of three films, and every point is the meeting of four lines. All that endless variety is based on one plan.

Figure 153 is a photograph of froth. In order to isolate one junction from the others and examine it in detail, you can make a wire tetrahedron like that in Figure 154*a* and dip it in the soap solution. When you withdraw it, the films automatically run from the wires inward to the center of the frame where they come together at a single point. That is the constant junction in the froth. That arrangement of films around a center point uses the smallest amount of material to interconnect the wires. You can easily calculate, for ex-

b

ample, that the arrangement uses only 82% of the material that would be used to enclose three out of the four exterior faces of the frame.

Close to the corners of the wire frame, three films join one another at 120° to form a straight line. But what happens at the center where four lines meet? With a little trigonometry, you can verify that the angle between any two lines at the center has a cosine of $-\frac{1}{3}$. Consequently the angle is 109° 28′ 16″.

What a strange angle! 109° 28′ 16″. It is as incommensurable as the angle of 137° 30′ 28″ that we used to lay out the points in the array of Figure 132a to describe phyllotaxis. We found, however, that the plant need never align stalks at that angle; we ourselves introduce the angle in order to make a two-dimensional diagram describe a three-dimensional pattern of growth. Here in the soap films, the situation is different. The angle of 109° 28′ 16″ really does occur at the center of the tetrahedral frame. Not only that, the angle has occurred at every four-way corner in every froth since the world began.

You may be disturbed by the materialization of such a queer and incommensurable angle. Certainly the ancient Pythagoreans would have been. They felt, for instance, that the diagonal of a square, being incommensurate with its edge, was a sin committed by the Great Architect and they swore themselves to secrecy regarding the fault lest His wrath be visited upon them. The Platonist philosopher Proclus repeats the story.

The people who first divulged the secret of the irrational numbers perished in a shipwreck to the last man, because the inexpressible, the formless, must be kept absolutely secret; those who divulged it and depicted this image of life perished instantaneously and will be tossed about by the waves for all eternity.

An interesting parallel to Pythagorean ideas about incommensurability is found in the latter-day words of Buckminster Fuller describing nature's use of pi:

I wondered "to how many decimal places does nature carry out *pi* before she decides that the computation can't be concluded?" Next I wondered, "to how many arbitrary decimal places does nature carry out the transcendental irrational before she decides to say it's a bad job and call it off?" If nature used *pi* she has to do what we call *fudging* of her design which means improvising, compromisingly. I thought sympathetically of nature's having to make all those myriad frustrated decisions each time she made a bubble. I didn't see how she managed to formulate the wake of every ship while managing the rest of the universe if she had to make all those decisions.

Fortunately for nature, the Pythagorean nightmare never materializes. Nature never compares the diagonal of a square with its edge to discover irrationality; she never compares the circumference of a circle with its diameter to learn of the transcendental nature of pi; and she certainly does not compute the cosine of −⅓ to get an angle of 109° 28′ 16″. Nature simply lets the molecules play however they may, and three films pulling equally against one another so they meet at 120° is not different from four lines of films pulling equally against one another so they meet at 109° 28′ 16″. For nature, one of those angles is as easy to make as the other.

Let us see how that incommensurable angle arises in other situations. Suppose you dip the wire frame with its films once again into the soap solution. This time, when you withdraw it, a spherical tetrahedron sits in the middle, as shown in Figure 154*b*. Again, all the films meet three by three at 120°, and the lines they form meet four by four at about 109.5°. The films are the minimum that can interconnect the wires and contain the central bubble.

If you dip a wire cube into the solution, the films do not join in a single point at the center. Instead, they make a square partition with slightly curved edges, as revealed in Figure 155*a*. When you dip and withdraw the cubical frame a second time, additional

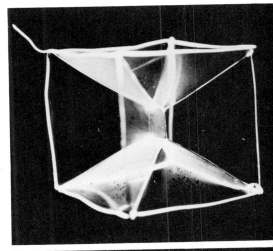

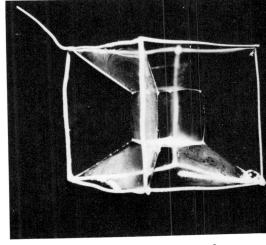

b

films join the square at the center to make the spherical cube shown in frame *b*. Once again, the films join in lines three at a time and the lines join at points four at a time, so that the films meet the frame and support the central bubble with the least possible material.

It is especially interesting to observe that the regular four-way corner of 109.5°, which the films spontaneously produce, precludes the making of a regular froth of regular cells. If you examine the regular and semiregular polyhedrons of Figures 5 and 6, you find none with face angles of 109.5°. None of them is isomorphic with cells in a froth. The one that comes closest to having the correct angle is the regular dodecahedron with its twelve pentagonal faces depicted at the bottom of Figure 5. It has face angles of 108°, and **Edwin B. Matzke**, who examined with a binocular dissecting microscope six hundred bubbles in the center of the most uniform froth he could make, found that 8% of them were irregular pentagonal dodecahedrons. As we learned in Chapter 1, however, no packing of polyhedrons with pentagonal faces can uniformly fill all of space, and consequently we can never hope to find a froth made solely of pentagonal dodecahedrons.

Thinking about nature's difficulty in making a regular froth, Lord Kelvin came up with a most attractive suggestion. He saw that the truncated octahedron shown in Figure 6 (the second polyhedron from the left in the top row), which has eight hexagonal faces and six square faces, has at each vertex two angles of 120° and one angle of 90°, so that the average angle at a vertex is 110° — very close to the required 109.5°. Furthermore, as illustrated in Figure 7, truncated octahedrons, unlike pentagonal dodecahedrons, pack with themselves to uniformly fill space. Kelvin reasoned that by distorting the basic form slightly, he could make the angles exact. The polyhedron could then serve as the repetitive cell of a perfectly uniform froth. Apparently, however, nature has never heeded his suggestion. In the six hundred cells that Matzke examined, he found no truncated octahedrons.

Part of the problem was that Matzke could not get the bubbles to stack in the same way that truncated octahedrons stack. Each new bubble that is added to a froth immediately takes up the most advantageous position; it does not wait until other bubbles are in place so that they can all adjust together. Conceivably, if bubbles stayed where they are first formed, we would find truncated octahedrons in the dishpan, but for now, nature's creation is far from Kelvin's ideal.

A more rewarding approach to the description of the cell in a froth can be found in statistical averages. As explained more fully in the notes to this chapter, a polygon that has face angles of 109° 28′ 16″ must have 5.104 edges and, in order to make a polyhedron, 13.394 of those polygons must join at 22.789 corners. Those relations are the mathematical manifestation of spatial constraints. They follow from the fact that the films link up with one another in space to form continuous three-dimensional networks.

Of course, a single cell with those average properties is impossible to realize; you cannot make a polygon that has .104 parts of an edge or a polyhedron with .789 parts of a corner. Unlike the angles or the value of pi with which we were earlier concerned, edges, polygons, and corners come in integral amounts: you either have an edge or a corner or you do not. Statistically, however, as an average of many bubbles in many froths, the "typical" cell can be realized. And in fact it is. If, like Matzke, you examine a few hundred bubbles in a froth, you will indeed find that they have, on the average, 5 to 6 edges per face, 13 to 14 faces, and 22 to 23 corners.

The lesson is that the regular corners, which inevitably result from the molecules pulling themselves together as closely as possible, preclude the making of a uniform froth in which all the cells are identical. Since the constraints of space prohibit the existence of a single cell with all the right properties, nature combines many cells with many different properties and gets the average to come out right. In the end, the blind molecules achieve a regular order.

The Mathematics of Bubbles

UNLIKE BUBBLES enmeshed in a froth, free-floating bubbles are spherical. That is not surprising because a sphere has the smallest amount of surface of any enclosure. The shrinking of the film to form a sphere is like the shrinking of the film to form a three-way junction between three thumbtacks: both configurations use the least material in the given situation.

When a spherical bubble falls on a flat surface, such as a wet sheet of glass, it transforms itself into a hemisphere. Under those conditions, when the bubble can take advantage of the glass to help enclose its air, the hemisphere rather than the sphere has the least surface in relation to its volume. Let us look closely at what happens when the sphere is transformed into a hemisphere. In particular, let us examine the relations of the volumes, radii, pressures, and areas in those two enclosures. Such a comparison involves some mathematics, but the simplicity of the relations among the mathematical symbols underlines the simple way that surface tension produces different geometric configurations.

When the spherical bubble changes to a hemisphere on landing on a sheet of glass, it neither increases nor decreases its supply of air. In other words, the volume of the original sphere equals the volume of the hemisphere, so that

$$\frac{4}{3} \pi r_S{}^3 = \frac{1}{2} (\frac{4}{3} \pi r_H{}^3)$$

where r_S and r_H are the radii of the sphere and the hemisphere. That formula reduces to

$$r_S = (\frac{1}{2})^{\frac{1}{3}} r_H$$

which states that the radius of the sphere is 79% ($= 100 \times (\frac{1}{2})^{\frac{1}{3}}$) of the radius of the hemisphere.

Next we need to know that the pressure in a soap

bubble is inversely proportional to its radius. That proportionality means that greater pressure exists in a small bubble than in a large one. Think about that statement for a moment. Is it not obviously wrong? Everyone knows, for example, that if you put air into an automobile tire, the tire expands and the pressure increases. In contrast, though, when you put air into a bubble, the bubble expands and the pressure decreases. Can both statements be correct?

Yes. Tires behave differently from bubbles; they do not expand as much. The rubber is not as elastic as the soap film and so it allows stresses to build up. In contrast, the soap film never exerts itself beyond the force of six-thousandths of an ounce per inch. That force is the same for thin skins and thick skins, for big bubbles and small bubbles. A bubble simply expands until the force exerted by the air inside exactly balances the pull within the skin of six-thousandths of an ounce per inch.

The idea that there is low pressure in big bubbles makes sense when you experiment with a segment of film. Figure 156a shows that when the pressure on the two sides of a film is the same, the film runs straight. Frame b reveals that if you blow with a light pressure on the straight film, it deflects slightly and has a radius of curvature of r_2. In frame c you learn that blowing with more pressure bends the film more sharply so that it has a radius of curvature of r_1. Bubbles are shaped by internal pressure in exactly the same way, so that the smaller the bubble, that is to say, the smaller the radius of curvature, the greater is the internal pressure. We have already found that the ratio of the radius of the sphere to the hemisphere is $(\frac{1}{2})^{\frac{1}{3}}$, that is to say,

$$\frac{r_S}{r_H} = (\frac{1}{2})^{\frac{1}{3}}$$

Since the pressure is inversely proportional to the radius, we now know that

$$\frac{P_H}{P_S} = (\frac{1}{2})^{\frac{1}{3}}$$

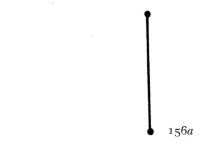
156a

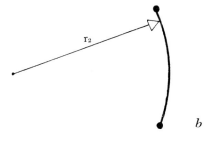
b

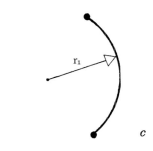
c

where P_H is the pressure in the hemisphere and P_S is the pressure in the sphere.

We can also calculate the ratio between A_H, the area of the film in the hemisphere, and A_S, the area of the film in the sphere. We find that

$$\frac{A_H}{A_S} = \frac{2\pi r_H^2}{4\pi r_S^2}$$

and since

$$\frac{A_H}{A_S} = \frac{r_S^2}{2^{\frac{1}{3}}} \times \frac{1}{r_S^2}$$

then

$$\frac{A_H}{A_S} : \left(\frac{1}{2}\right)^{\frac{1}{3}}$$

Thus the area of the film in the hemisphere is less than the area of the film in the sphere in the same proportion as the pressure in the hemisphere is less than the pressure in the sphere.

The summary of that juggling of symbols is given by the elegant statement

$$\frac{r_S}{r_H} : \frac{P_H}{P_S} : \frac{A_H}{A_S} : \left(\frac{1}{2}\right)^{\frac{1}{3}}$$

showing the relations of radii, pressures, and areas. Even those who find mathematics difficult can enjoy deriving such a result, for the mathematics describes far better than words the unequivocal relations among geometry and forces in the transformation of a bubble.

Let us look at some other transformations. If part of the hemispherical bubble rests upon an inclined plane, it will ascend the plane, dragging the rest of the bubble behind it like a wooden leg, until the center of curvature lies at the joint between the inclined plane and the horizontal surface. Figure 157 shows cross sections of bubbles that have dragged themselves into progressively narrower corners. All the bubbles in the figure have the same volume and their cross sections are drawn to scale. We discover that their radii become longer as the corners become

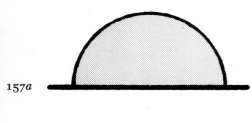

157*a*

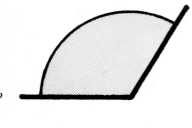

b

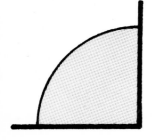

c

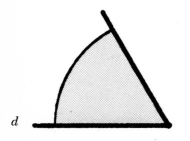

d

more cramped. At the same time, the surface areas of the bubbles and their pressures decrease.

When a hemisphere is compared to its parent sphere, we have seen that the radii, pressures, and surfaces are related as $(\frac{1}{2})^{\frac{1}{3}}$. When one-third of a sphere, as in frame b, is compared to the same parent sphere, those ratios are as $(\frac{1}{3})^{\frac{1}{3}}$, whereas the ratios for a quadrant of a sphere and the sixth part of a sphere, as shown in frames c and d, are as $(\frac{1}{4})^{\frac{1}{3}}$ and $(\frac{1}{6})^{\frac{1}{3}}$. Thus the radii, pressures, and areas are related in a very simple manner: as the cube root of whatever fraction the part of the sphere bears to the whole.

The driving force behind the regular changes in radii, pressures, and areas is still the play of particles getting sucked into and squeezed out of the interior of the film. It seems most remarkable that such orderly mathematical transformations are created by aggregations of agitated particles. But since none of the particles want to stay on the surfaces of the film, the surfaces shrink and the curvature straightens out. The straightening of curvature results in a lengthening of the radius of curvature and a corresponding reduction in pressure. The big picture is determined by the interactions of the tiny pieces. Form is born of the formless struggle of molecules.

Now if you set two hemispherical bubbles on wet glass, they will draw close together and simultaneously build a wall between themselves. Figure 158 shows, in cross section, how the wall develops. We see that the films of the two hemispheres in the top of the figure are not in equilibrium with each other; they touch tangentially instead of making a full-fledged 120° junction. But observe what happens at the point of tangency. When the two films with their four surfaces meet (remember that each film has both an inside and outside surface), the molecules jump into a single film with two surfaces and bring into existence the intermediate partition. Two films become one; four surfaces become two, and as the single film grows, the other films sidle over to join it at 120°.

Even with an intermediate partition, the film area in the double bubble is less than the film area in the two

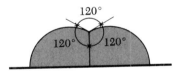

158

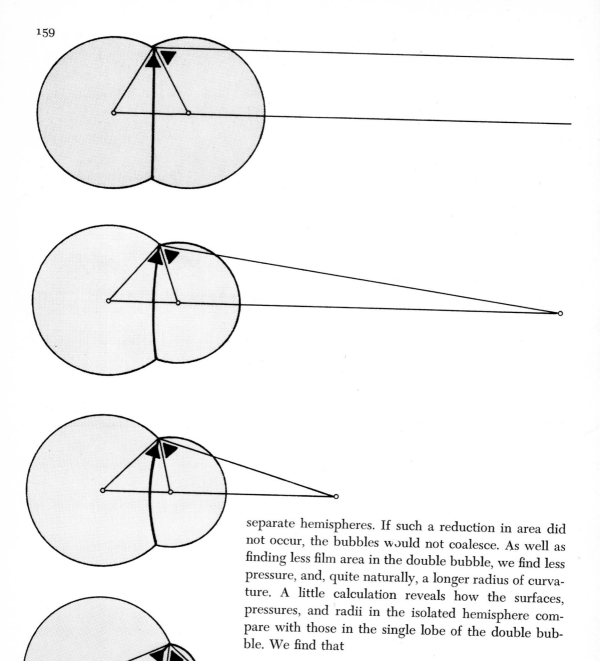

separate hemispheres. If such a reduction in area did not occur, the bubbles would not coalesce. As well as finding less film area in the double bubble, we find less pressure, and, quite naturally, a longer radius of curvature. A little calculation reveals how the surfaces, pressures, and radii in the isolated hemisphere compare with those in the single lobe of the double bubble. We find that

$$\frac{r_H}{r_D} : \frac{P_D}{P_H} : \frac{A_D}{A_H} : \left(\frac{27}{32}\right)^{\frac{1}{3}}$$

where r_H, P_H, and A_H are the radius, pressure, and area of the hemisphere, and r_D, P_D, and A_D are the

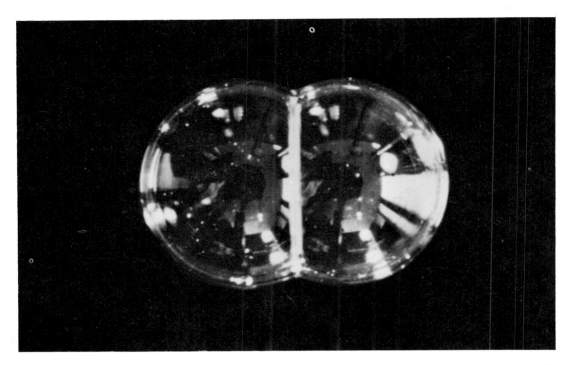

radius, pressure, and area of one lobe of the double bubble. If you remember to include the area of the intermediate partition, you will see the fraction $^{27}\!/_{32}$ come about quite naturally.

The top diagram of Figure 159 shows a view of the top of the double bubble. Since the radii of the two lobes are equal, the pressures are equal, and the intermediate partition runs straight. The figure jibes with the photograph of the double bubble in Figure 160. However, if two unequal bubbles join, the intermediate partition blows into the large bubble where the pressure is less. We can see in the three lower diagrams of Figure 159 that the deformation of the intermediate partition increases as the inequality between the lobes increases.

The deformation of the intermediate partition takes place in a most logical manner. Like most of what we know about soap bubbles, the laws regarding that deformation were discovered by the Belgian physicist J. A. F. Plateau, whose great work, *Statique Expéri-*

mentale et Théorique des Liquides, was published thirty years after he became permanently blind, so that during those many years he saw his experiments only through the eyes of others.

Figure 159, adapted from Plateau's work, shows a remarkable fact about the geometry of bubble clusters. In each frame two 60° angles are marked by small solid triangles. Their existence is necessitated by the fact that the films meet at 120°. Observe the locations of the 60° angles; one marks the position of the triple junction relative to the centers of curvature of the two lobes, and the other marks the position of the triple junction relative to the center of curvature of the smaller lobe and the center of curvature of the partition. It is obvious from the figure that the three centers of curvature lie on the same straight line. Knowing those geometrical facts, you can easily spell out the relations among the radii. You can determine, for example, that the square of the distance between the centers of the bubbles is equal to the sum of the two radii squared, less their product; that is to say,

$$d^2 = r_1{}^2 + r_2{}^2 - r_1 r_2$$

To prove that relation, all you need to know is a little plane geometry. You may also be able to prove that the radius of curvature of the intermediate partition is the product of the radii of the lobes divided by their difference; that is,

$$r_P = \frac{r_1 r_2}{r_2 - r_1}$$

or, even more simply, that

$$\frac{1}{r_1} = \frac{1}{r_2} + \frac{1}{r_P}$$

You can thus see algebraically, as well as geometrically, that nothing is left to chance in the joining of the bubbles. Every junction, every curvature, and the length of every partition is determined absolutely by the random motions of the molecules elbowing their way into the centers of the films.

Plateau discovered that the geometrical relations in

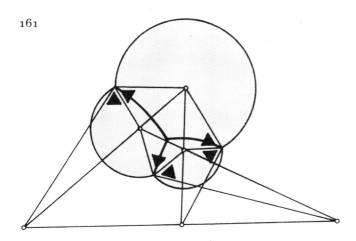

161

the double bubble hold for larger clusters as well. Figure 161 shows a triple bubble. The 60° angles are again marked with solid triangles and again we see that the radius of curvature of the partition between any two of the lobes lies on the line through the centers of those lobes. Furthermore, the three radii of curvature of the three intermediate partitions lie on a straight line of their own. As in the double bubble, we can determine distances between the centers of the lobes, we can observe that the higher pressures in the small lobes push the partitions into the largest lobe, and we can calculate that the total area of the skin of the cluster is the minimum necessary to enclose and separate the three quantities of air. All elements are fully specified. We can check the curvatures and dimensions algebraically or, more simply, we can lay a sheet of glass holding a real bubble cluster over the diagram of the bubble cluster and see that the real cluster and the diagram match in all respects. Figure 162 shows a three-lobed cluster that is similar to the diagram of Figure 161.

In larger clusters too, algebraic descriptions accompany the geometric configurations. Just as the average cell of the froth approaches a regular and definable form — although any particular cell can take a variety of shapes — so too the average action of the molecules produces well-defined forms — although the

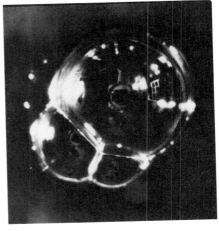

162

path of any particular molecule is unpredictable. Among molecules, collective action swamps the indeterminacy of the individual and produces both visual and mathematical beauty.

8

Packing and Cracking

WE HAVE SEEN that three-way 120° joints occur when boundaries or interfaces are minimized as in the turtle's shell, in froth, or in grains of a crystal. The same pattern emerges when groups of similar objects pack together as closely as possible and when a homogeneous material splits into separate pieces.

Close Packing

SPHERICAL OBJECTS like marbles or billiard balls can pack together on a flat surface to form several regular arrangements. In particular, they can join in the square and the triangular arrays shown in Figure 163. The square array in frames *a* and *c* describes the packing of bottles in a rack or eggs in a carton; the triangular or close-packed array in frame *c* describes the packing of billiard balls illustrated in Figure 164.

Balls packed in the square array group less closely than in the triangular array. We realize that fact if we mentally slide a row in the square array one-half the diameter of a ball to the right or left. The balls that are moved slip into the gaps between the balls in the adjacent rows. Interlocking all the rows in this fashion necessarily brings all the balls closer together — in a close-packed or triangular arrangement. Molecules join each other in that close-packed arrangement to make crystals, just as round leafstalks fill each other's gaps to produce spiral phyllotaxis.

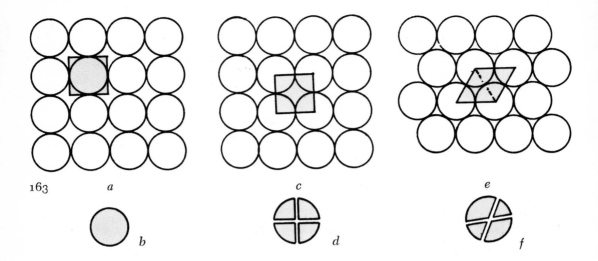

163   *a*   *c*   *e*

b   *d*   *f*

164

You can compare the closeness of the arrays in Figure 163 by comparing the sizes of the boxes necessary to enclose exactly one sphere. Because all the spheres are the same size, you might suppose that regardless of how they are arranged each sphere would fit the same box. That is not at all the case — especially if you enforce the rule that the boxes must stack neatly with each other without any waste of space.

The boxes you can use are known to crystallographers as unit cells, and the unit cell for the square array turns out to be a cube, the cross section of which is the shaded square of Figure 163*a*. Other cubes can be joined with the one shown so that each cube encloses exactly one sphere and all the cubes together cover the whole plane with no space left over. That is all quite clear for the unit cell as drawn in frame *a*. But now look at frame *c*. Here the same unit cell is drawn, but it is located differently. It cuts four pieces from four different spheres. Those pieces can be reassembled, however, as shown in frame *d*, to make one sphere, and thus the definition of the unit cell is preserved: it is still the "box" that encloses one sphere.

The unit cell for the close-packed or triangular array is a parallelepiped whose cross section (a parallelogram crossed with a dotted diagonal line to show that it is composed of two triangles) is shown in frame *e*. We see again that the four pieces of the four different spheres can be rearranged to make exactly one sphere and that the parallelepiped can be reproduced and stacked with itself to enclose all the spheres.

Now, the interesting point is that the volume of the unit cell in the square array is $8r^3$, where r is the radius of a sphere, whereas the volume of the unit cell in the close-packed array is only $4\sqrt{3}\,r^3$. Thus, spheres in the close-packed array fit into a space that is 87% $[= 100 \times (4\sqrt{3}/8)]$ of the space needed to house spheres in the square array. Accordingly, we have described the greater closeness of the close-packed array with a definite number.

If you make real arrangements with marbles, you find it quite difficult to get them to stack in a square array. They persist in rolling into the valleys between their neighbors. They persist in packing more closely. We can describe the propensity of marbles to roll into valleys in terms of energy, for just as we say that raindrops have less potential energy when they sit in the valleys rather than on the tops of mountains, we can say that marbles have less potential energy when they sit in the valleys rather than on the tops of other marbles. Consequently, if the marbles are free to move, they will automatically adopt a pattern of minimum energy.

And the three-way junctions — how do they arise? Note how three marbles in the close-packed array surround every leftover space or interstice (Figure 163e). If those marbles have soft or deformable walls like balloons or lumps of clay or plant cells, and they all expand simultaneously (or the entire array is squeezed), each of the three will fill a third of the interstice, so that in the center of every interstice, the three will meet at a single point. Thus the expansion of close-packed units automatically produces a network of triple junctions.

You can see how a similar expansion of units in the square array produces four-way junctions. But any slippage, any movement of those units into a configuration with less energy, makes triple corners.

We see the deformation of units and the development of triple junctions in Figure 165 in kernels of

e

f

g

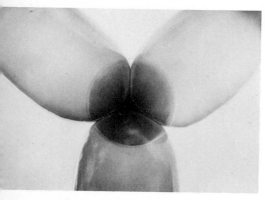

166

167

sweet corn (*a*), in the cob of the *Zamia skinneri*, (*b*) (photographed at Fairchild Tropical Gardens in Miami, Florida), barnacles (*c*), yeast rolls fresh from the pan (*d*), segments of onion (*e*), domains of coral polyps (*f*), and cells in the nest of a wasp (*g*). All those cells push and get pushed by their neighbors so that they pack together three by three as closely as possible.

It is interesting to observe how much the junctions of the onion in frame *e* look like partitions in a froth of bubbles. For example, the smaller lobe of the double kernel in the lower left presses into the larger lobe, just as the smaller lobe presses into the larger lobe of a double bubble.

In three dimensions, too, forms arising from close packing resemble those brought about by the entirely different force of surface tension. If you interlock two balloons by crimping their centers and twisting them around one another, they spontaneously make a three-dimensional four-way tetrahedral joint, as shown in Figure 166 — the same joint made by the soap films in the tetrahedral frame of Figure 154*a*.

In the photograph of the balloons, we look through three of the arms to see the fourth extending beyond. The junction of balloons does not come about because their surfaces flow together to form a system of partitions with a minimum of material. Instead, each half of each balloon presses equally against the others and they all stand at angles of 109.5° to one another. In the same vein, note how the kernels in the plastic foam (polystyrene) of Figure 167 look like bubbles in a froth. Again we see that close packing and surface tension produce similar forms.

Cracking

Now, CONSIDER an entirely different phenomenon, cracking. Observe the rock in Figure 168*a* that has split into three pieces. Assuming that the rock is homogeneous throughout — that it did not crack where it did because of inherent weaknesses — we can suppose that as the stress built up, the molecular bonds within the stone stretched like elastic bands pulling this way and that in a continually adjusting balance of strain, and that, finally, when the stress got too great, the rock shattered around a triple node. For an elastic material (like rock!) rupture occurs suddenly and proceeds out of 120° joints. Figure 168*b* shows similar three-way cracks in mud.

Let us compare that cracking with the cracking of an inelastic material such as the glaze on a piece of pottery. (See Figure 169.) In the glaze the molecular bonds do not yield and make adjustments as the stress builds up. The rupture occurs right where the stress arises, first in one section and then in another. By observing the lengths of the cracks and noting which ones pass through others and which are interrupted, you can, to a large extent, determine the order in which the fissures occurred.

That sequential pattern of cracking in the glaze is characterized by right-angle joints. The explanation for the occurrence of right angles is quite simple: because the cracks release all the stress in one direction — parallel to themselves — they can only be joined by cracks that run in the opposite direction — perpendicularly.

Close inspection of the photograph shows that some 120° joints also occur in the glaze. Usually they occur in portions that have been previously isolated by cracks on all sides. That isolation frees the glaze so that its stresses can make elastic adjustments and the cracks can join in threes. Thus the rule stands: cracking in elastic materials occurs suddenly, around 120° joints; cracking in inelastic material occurs sequentially, and new cracks join old ones at 90°.

Consequently, films and cracks have a great deal in common. Films that are elastic, like films of soap and water, shift in relation to one another to meet at 120° — just like cracks; films that cannot deform their boundaries meet those boundaries at 90° — just like cracks. The overall pattern made by films is one of minimum energy or exposure of surface, and again the

b

169

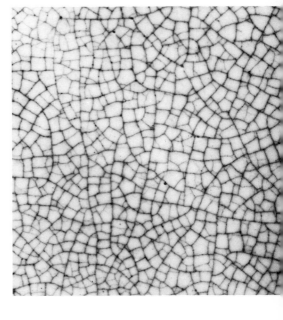

same is true of cracks. By way of contrast, however, the film is the material between the voids and is formed by particles getting pulled into it, whereas the crack is the void within the material and is formed by particles getting pulled out of it. The interesting point is that although the film and the crack are formed by entirely different mechanisms, they frequently look the same.

Let us now consider some more complicated patterns of cracks.

Figure 170 shows the cracking of the bark of trees. In frame *a* we see the trunk of a Washington palm (*Washington robusta*) that splits into longitudinal fissures as the inner core expands. In the Melaleuca of frame *b* the bark "explodes," whereas in the live oak (*Quercus virginiana*) and the yellow pine of frames *c* and *d* the bark splits into separate cells or scales. The molecular forces within the bark of trees is different for each species so that the forced expansion of that bark produces different patterns. In addition to splitting the existing bark, the growth of the tree adds new bark, and that piling up of new material also affects the final appearance. Nature seldom sticks to simple one-force systems. Her forms usually represent the equilibrium of several forces, the balance of several compulsions. To analyze the effects of one force is easy; to analyze the interplay of two or more forces is next to impossible. But nature, oblivious to our analytical difficulties, freely mixes her compulsions to create the whole spectrum of form and pattern.

Geologic Analogies

A GOOD EXAMPLE of the complexity of form that arises from the interaction of simple forces is the pattern of cracks that develops in poster paint that has been spread on glass. Because the interior of the paint dries more slowly than the exterior, the simple patterns of 90° and 120° joints are distorted. It turns out, however, that many of the patterns that arise in a layer of

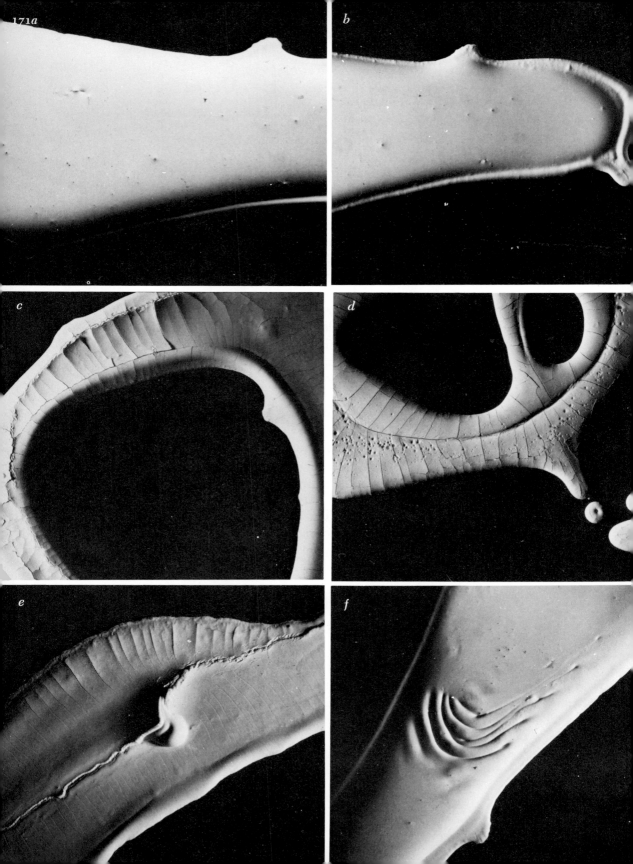

paint are similar to those that arise in the earth's crust — despite the enormous difference in their sizes.

We need not be surprised at the analogy of paint and the earth's crust when we remember that if the earth with its liquid core was reduced to the size of a bubble or a drop, its crust — the hard rock surface that we know — would have the thickness of a thin film. If the earth were reduced to the size of an orange, it would not feel like an orange at all; it would feel soft and squishy like a tomato.

Figure 171 shows different stages in the drying of poster paint. Frame *a* shows how the drying starts at the extreme edge of the blob where the paint meets the glass. The drying at the edge sets a firm boundary and, as drying continues, that boundary cannot shrink further: it can only crack. In frame *b* we see how the progressive drying of the surface of the paint pushes a roll of wet material away from the boundary toward the center of the blob. As depicted in frame *c,* however, the drying often leaps over the roll to form an interior plateau. Note also that fissures can develop along the tops of the rolls. Those fissures come about when the wet material inside the roll gets sucked back toward the edges that have already dried. Frame *d* shows a central fissure with secondary cracks running perpendicularly between it and the boundaries. We also see the central collapse of individual drops of paint. Again, the already dry perimeter of the drop draws wetness to it away from the center, so that a dimple develops in the center — much like the dimple in a kernel of dried corn. If you turn the glass upside down as the paint dries, you can verify that the dimples and fissures do not come about because of gravitational collapse; you will see the same holes and crevices, even though the force of gravity works directly against their development. Frame *d* shows some pits that are formed as bubbles in the hardened surface release their gas. Those pits differ from the dimples: the pits are like volcanic vents; the dimples are like sink holes.

Frame *e* illustrates still another geological event. The drying and collapse of the plateaus force the wet material below the surface up and out of the central cleft, just as hot lava gets forced out of vents in the earth's crust. The last frame shows the folding of the skin when lateral forces operate — when, for example, the glass is held vertically while the paint dries.

Consequently, we find that a difference in shrinkage between the skin and the interior of a blob of paint no longer leads to simple patterns of 90° and 120° cracks, but produces instead many of the complicated patterns that we find in geological processes. Both the skin of the paint and the skin of the earth are fixed in absolute size. Both skins crack and deform because of the movement of liquid below their surfaces.

The geologist A. J. Bull used an interesting analogy to demonstrate that the earth's crust was fixed in size, that it had not shrunk overly much. He coated an inflated rubber balloon with gelatin and observed how the gelatin puckered when the balloon contracted. In the dried peas of Figure 172 we see the same three-way puckered joints that Bull observed in the gelatin on his balloon. Like the gelatin, the skin of the pea shrinks as much as possible, that is, it withdraws and leaves puckered ridges that are as small in area as possible. Those ridges that get left behind join in a network of three-way junctions, just like the residue of scalded milk in Figure 148a. From the absence of triple junctions in the main mountain chains of the world, Bull concluded that "the structures of the earth's crust have not been produced by a general contraction."

Twelve years prior to Bull's balloon experiment, Alfred Wegener proposed a radically different theory about the earth's history. Wegener believed that the earth had remained about the same size, but he supposed that the continents had floated across its surface like the scum on boiling soup. At one time in the earth's history, all the continents fitted together to form a supercontinent, Pangea, or "all land," and Pangea floated in the middle of a superocean, Panthalassa, or "all sea."

After years of neglect, Wegener's theory has found wide acceptance. Figure 173 (redrawn from Dietz, 1970) is a modern interpretation of how Pangea

172

looked 200 million years ago. Fragments of that super-continent are the continents we know today: *a*, North America; *b*, Asia; *c*, South America; *d*, Africa; *e*, India; *f*, Antarctica; and *g*, Australia.

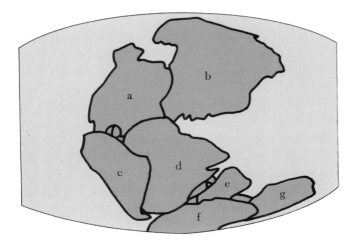

173

At the beginning of the age of the dinosaurs, chunks of the earth's crust converged to form Pangea. At the end of the reign of the dinosaurs and the beginning of the reign of mammals, that single continent fragmented, and its chunks drifted across the surface of the earth on plates or crustal rafts, forty to sixty miles thick — the relative thickness of a tomato skin on a tomato.

The plates and continents are still moving. They may be driven by swirling turbulence of material within the earth and by the rotation of the earth, for like the atmosphere, the plates do not keep pace with the earth's rotation; they drift steadily backwards, that is to say, to the west. Within your lifetime, for example, the entire North American continent will drift westward the length of your body.

Although we do not understand fully the mechanisms that drive the plates, we can appreciate the enormous distances some of them have traveled. In Pangea, as depicted in Figure 173, India and Australia adhered directly to Antarctica. India broke loose first and migrated northward to crash into Asia and thrust up the Himalaya Mountains. Australia engages now in a similar northward trek. The movement of North and South America away from Asia and Africa created the entire Atlantic Ocean. New sea floor oozed up out of the rift between those continental plates like the poster paint out of the crack depicted in Fig. 171e. It is estimated that each year 50 billion tons of new land push up from the rifts in the earth's crust. Iceland, for example, increases steadily in size as new land flows out of the rift in the middle of the Atlantic Ocean. The fresh material joins the edges of the separating plates so that they increase in size like the plates in the turtle's shell shown in Figure 149b.

Figure 173 holds special interest for us because the cracks of Pangea join in the triple junctions that typify a homogeneous material that is uniformly stressed. Furthermore, because we can assume that all the plates meet three at a time to form a sphere, we can make use of the topological formulas that describe the spatial relations among the parts of the polyhedrons pictured in Figures 5 and 6. We learn thereby that 1, the number of triple nodes that define the pattern of the plates can be related to N, the number of plates, by the formula

$$2(N - 2)$$

2, the edges of all the plates add up to

$$3(N - 2)$$

and 3, the edges of the average plate add up to

$$\frac{6(N - 2)}{N}$$

Consequently, through the use of those formulas, that is to say, through knowledge of the limitations of spatial arrangements, we can reconstruct the entire pattern of plates from only a few bits and pieces.

Returning for a moment to Bull's junctions of gelatin on the balloon, it is interesting to learn that, although they did not depict patterns of mountain chains, the biologist W. E. Le Gros Clark found that they recalled "in a striking way" the wrinkles on the surface of the human brain. The analogy that failed to fit the earth's crust fitted man's brain instead.

Of course, the wrinkles in the gelatin or on the skin of the pea come about because the surface contracts. Has man's brain contracted and wrinkled? No, the wrinkles on the surface of the brain face inward like valleys rather than outward like ridges. The surface of the brain has not shrunk. It has expanded, and forced the valleys, the parts that have been left behind during that expansion, into a pattern of three-way junctions. Man's brain is like a pea turned inside out.

As another example, Figure 174 shows the scars of three-way wrinkles on the shell of the horseshoe crab. Before the crab molts, its new shell, underneath its old shell, is wrinkled, like the skin of a water-soaked finger. After the shedding of the old shell, the new shell fills out and stiffens, and only the scars remain to tell of its wrinkled state. In the tail shown in frame *b*, we see that the wrinkles, although arising from three-way junctions in the center, join the relatively stiff boundary at 90°. No strain is present parallel to the boundary so the wrinkles join it perpendicularly.

Many Causes

HERE IN REVIEW are the agencies that give rise to the pattern of three-way joints: surface tension as with soap bubbles, close packing as with buns in a pan, cracking as in mud, and wrinkling as in the human brain. With so many different mechanisms producing the same pattern, it is obviously impossible, on the basis of the pattern alone, to determine how it comes into existence. In Figure 175, for example, it is impossible to say why the fissures of the starfish line up three by three in the center of the body and perpendicularly at the boundary. Is cracking involved? The close packing of cells? Surface tension? Perhaps all those forces are at work. A similar pattern occurs in the

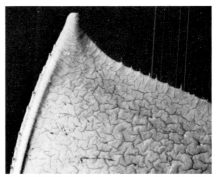

a

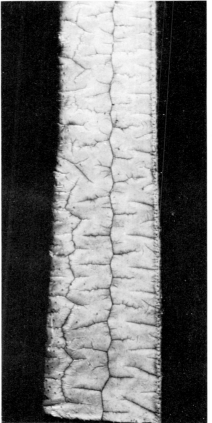

b

175*a*

b

c

d

starfish in frame *b*. And observe the pinecones and the fruit of the screw pine in the last two frames. Three-way corners again and again.

As another example of the difficulty of determining the origins of the pattern, look at Figure 176, which shows six examples of scales: *a*, the skin of a snake; *b*, the skin of a fish (a lobe-finned coelacanth photographed at the Harvard University Museum); *c*, the foot of a tortoise; *d*, the fused hairs of the ant-eating pangolin (photographed at the Harvard University Museum); *e*, seeds of milkweed; and *f*, feathers of the Java peacock (also photographed at the Harvard University Museum). Each scale, group of fused hairs, seed, or feather overlaps the joint between two others so that their edges meet in threes. All those "scales" serve different functions, and yet all are variations of the same triradiate theme.

But surface tension, close packing, cracking, and wrinkling — do they not have something in common that explains why they all produce the same pattern? In a sense, yes. The common element is that they all produce minimum surfaces. The particles of soap and water shrink into themselves, the expanding buns push one another into each other's gaps so that they minimize surface contacts, the cracks lay open the smallest amount of material, and the wrinkles are the minimum residue left behind after the rest has shrunk or expanded. The technical description for all those processes is the minimization of work or energy.

We thus see that the specific mechanism that brings a pattern or form into being is not as important to its overall appearance as how its constituent parts relate in space: if the parts are free to adjust and find equilibrium, they arrange themselves in a configuration of minimum energy. A slice or plane section through that configuration will reveal 120° junctions — not because nature is driven by a mysterious passion to create triradiate corners, but because three lines are the fewest that can be brought together at each point in the subdivision of a plane.

In those examples of minimum energy, the partitions, surfaces, cracks, and wrinkles push and pull

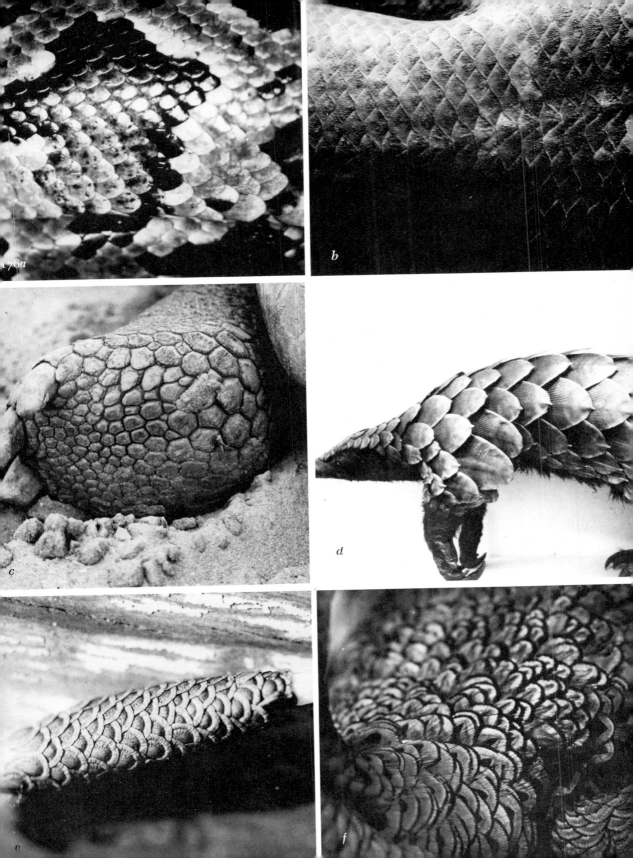

b

against one another until they find equilibrium in triple junctions. That pattern of junctions can come about even more directly, however, without any interaction among the parts; the pattern can arise simply because it is the most likely pattern to arise.

By way of example, Figure 177*a* shows how a sphere of chalk develops flat faces as it wears against the blackboard. The edges of those faces meet three at a time at each corner. Seldom will you find a four-way corner. Frame *b* explains why. It shows a piece of clay with portions sliced away so that five edges meet in two triple junctions. To get the edge in the middle to disappear so that four edges join in one junction, the slices have to be positioned precisely so that the two triple junctions coincide. If you take a shallow slice from the slope at the left or right, the two triple junctions move closer together and the intermediate edge shortens. If you take a deeper slice, the triple junctions will, in effect, pass through one another to generate another intermediate edge that runs at right angles to the existing one. The chances are that you will not be able to get the right depth of cut to make the two

178

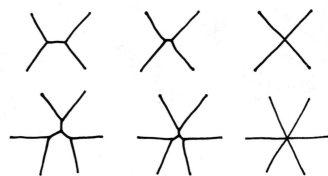

triple junctions meet precisely. And nature cannot do better. If a four-way junction occurs on the surface of the chalk, it degenerates quickly into two three-way junctions. Figure 178 indicates the precision with which three-way junctions must meet in order for four- or six-way junctions to occur. Two three-way junctions must meet precisely to make a four-way junction and

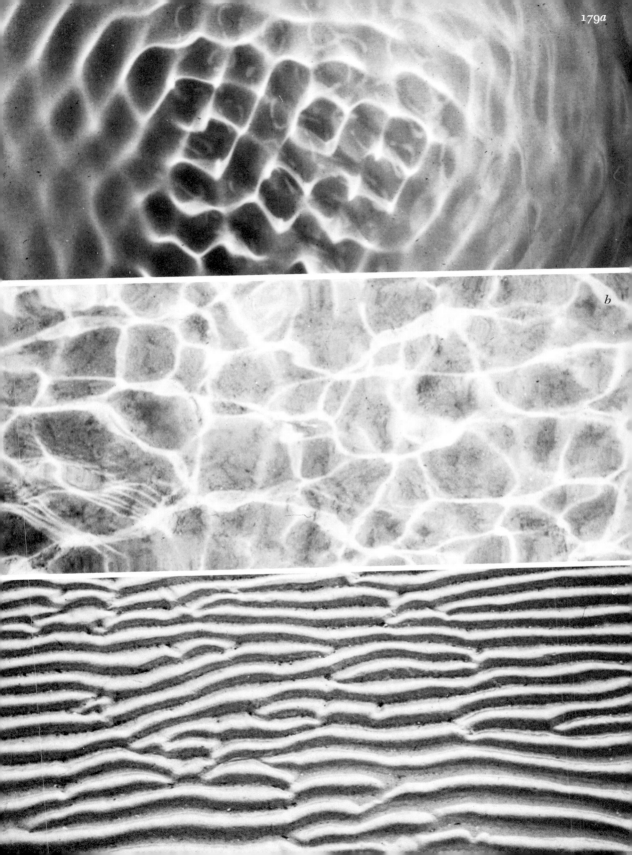

b

c

180

three three-way junctions must meet precisely to make a six-way junction.

Figure 179 shows that water in a pie plate that is vibrated at 510 cycles per second (*a*), the wind-rippled surface of a lake as reflected on the sandy bottom (*b*), and ripples in sand (*c*) are more likely to generate three-way than four-, five-, or six-way corners.

The schematic ripples in Figure 180 make the point even more clearly. When ridges, as represented by the dark lines, break at random locations as shown at the top, the valleys between them meet three at a time. To get four-way junctions of valleys, all the ridges must break along the same line, as shown at the bottom.

Consequently, we must add probability to our list of explanations for the occurrence of triple junctions. And in view of the variations of scales and feathers pictured in Figure 176, we had better consider evolution as an explanation as well. After all, is it not advantageous to have scales overlap so as to cover each other's joints? Is that not an adequate explanation for the similarity in appearance between the scales of the boa constrictor and the feathers of the sparrow?

Which explanation do we invoke to describe the markings of the zebra and the giraffes in Figure 181? Certainly those patterns must have had some kind of evolutionary advantage, but what specific physical mechanism brings them into existence? The junctions in the markings of the zebra look like ripples in sand. Perhaps they arise by chance. But the markings of the giraffe in frame *b* seem much too regular to attribute to chance. They look like a product of surface tension. But then again, how could surface tension produce the pattern on the giraffe in frame *c*? Are the mechanisms that produce the patterns necessarily the same for the two varieties of giraffe? We do not know. One of the great unsolved biological mysteries is how such patterns arise. They can have any number of different origins.

Any one of the three general explanations for the appearance and form of things — minimum energy, probability, and selective evolution — is sufficient to show why triple corners come into existence. Each of

a

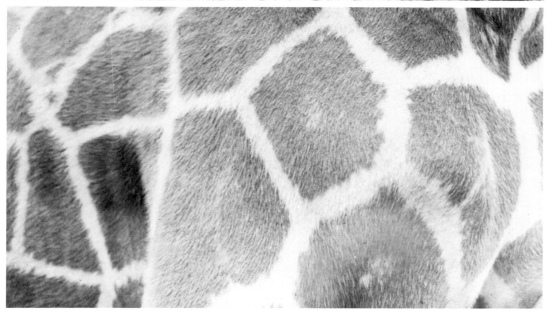

b

c

those explanations establishes independently the same pattern. Consequently, the pattern is overdetermined. We see it again and again, so that, as Leonardo da Vinci observed, nature appears finite.

Her finiteness arises because space prohibits so much and permits so little. In the same way that if nature requires direct flow to or from a central point, she must adopt the pattern of the explosion, and if she requires overall shortness as well as directness she must introduce branching, so, if she requires an economical network, she must use three-way joints. Again we find that nature cannot build anything she pleases in any way that she pleases. She must use patterns of hexagons, that is to say, three-way corners, in order to save material, and she must use other modules with those hexagons in order to enclose space. As we have seen before, she can never make a pentagonal snowflake. She can never make a regular icosahedral crystal. She cannot join a new crack with an old crack at any angle other than 90°. She must increase the surface area of a large organism if it is to function like a small organism. Growth of one part must affect growth of all parts.

The rules are rigorous, but within those rules variety abounds, and the rules show through the variations to portray a relatedness of parts that is aesthetically pleasing and a constancy of purpose that provides an eternal model for all of man's creations.

Chapter Notes

1

Space and Size

The Nature of Space

For a brief history of man's changing conceptions of space, see Sir Edward Whittaker, *From Euclid to Eddington* (New York: Dover, 1958). A description of the differing characteristics of Euclidean and non-Euclidean spaces is contained in Charles P. Steinmetz, *Four Lectures on Relativity and Space* (New York: Dover, 1967.)

For Wheeler's views, see John A. Wheeler, "Geometrodynamics," in Cecile M. DeWitt and John A. Wheeler, editors, *1967 Lectures in Mathematics and Physics, Battelle Rencontres* (New York: W. A. Benjamin, Inc., 1968); "Our Universe: The Known and the Unknown," *American Scientist* 56, no. 1 (1968): 1–20; the New York *Times*, February 5, 1967, p. E5; and April 4, 1971, p. E7.

Polyhedrons and Mosaics

Descriptions of the regular and semiregular mosaics and polyhedrons can be found in W. W. R. Ball, *Mathematical Recreations and Essays*, 11th ed. (Macmillan, London: 1959); and A. F. Wells, *The Third Dimension in Chemistry* (New York: Oxford University Press, 1956).

The fourteen semiregular polyhedrons of Figure 6 are the thirteen Archimedean polyhedrons, plus the "pseudorhombicuboctahedron" discovered by C. P. Miller and more recently described by V. G. Aškimuze.

The clustering of polyhedrons is described in Angelo Andreini's classic work, "Sulle reti di poliedri regolari e semiregolari e sull corispondenti reti correlative," *Memorie di Matematica e di Fisica della Società Italiana Delle Scienze,* (Rome: 1907), 14, ser. 3, 75–129.

The Effect of Scale

The most complete description of the effect of scale is still the second chapter of D'Arcy Thompson, *On Growth and Form*, 2nd ed. (Cambridge, England: At the University Press, 1942). The interested reader should also consult Bonner's work in John T. Bonner, *Morphogenesis* (New York: Atheneum, 1963); and "The Size of Life," *Natural History* 78, no. 1 (January 1969): 40–45.

Several references are made to F. W. Went, "The Size of Man," *American Scientist* 56, no. 4 1968), 400–413. Additional material with valuable references can be found in Stephen J. Gould, "Allometry and Size in Ontogeny and Phylogeny," *Biological Review* 41 (1966): 587–640.

Galileo's work is the well known *Two New Sciences,* translated by Henry Crew and Alfonso de Salvio (New York: Dover, 1954).

J. B. S. Haldane's words are found in "On Being the Right Size," in James R. Newman, *The World of Mathematics,* vol. 2, pp. 952–957 (New York: Simon and Schuster, 1956).

A good article on the growth of roots is Emanuel Epstein, "Roots," *Scientific American* 227, 5 (May 1973).

The data on heartbeats were compiled from a display at Boston's Museum of Science, the data on wingbeats from various sources, including David S. Smith, "The Flight Muscles of Insects," *Scientific American* 212, no. 6 (June 1965): 76–88; and A. V. Hill, "The Dimensions of Animals and Their Muscular Dynamics," *Science Progress* 38 (London, 1950): 209–230.

The latex casting of the human lung in Figure 13a was supplied by Michael Woldenberg of the Laboratory for Computer Graphics at Harvard University. The plastic cast of the arteries of the dog in Figure 13c is from a display at the Museum of Science in Boston, Massachusetts.

The photograph of the human tibia in Figure 19g taken by Carl Struve is reproduced by permission of Prestel-Verlag of Munich, Germany. The model of the space frame in Figure 19h is reproduced through the courtesy of Frei Otto of the Atelier Warmbronn, Warmbronn, Germany.

Ranko Bon's analysis of building shapes can be found in "Allometry in Micro-Environmental Morphology" (Harvard University, Laboratory of Computer Graphics: 1971).

2
Basic Patterns

The introductory quote is from Francis Bacon, "Of the Advancement of Learning," *The Works of Francis Bacon,* vol. 1, p. 104 (London: H. Bryer, 1803).

How branching patterns minimize overall length has been described by Luna B. Leopold, "Trees and Streams: The Efficiency of Branching Patterns," *Journal of Theoretical Biology* 31 (1971): 339–354.

For a more complete account of the mathematical analysis of branched networks, see A. Shimbel, "Structural Parameters of Communication Networks," *Bulletin of Mathematical Biophysics* 15 (1953): 501–507.

A new and rigorous presentation of the limited one- and two-dimensional symmetry groups can be found in Arthur L. Loeb, *Color and Symmetry* (New York: Wiley, 1971).

The photograph of the model of Antoni Gaudi's *Sagrada Familia* in Figure 27a is reproduced through the courtesy of Verlag Gerd Hatje of Stuttgart, Germany. The photograph of Frei Otto's structural model in Figure 27b is reproduced through the courtesy of Frei Otto of the Atelier Warmbronn, Warmbronn, Germany.

3
All Things Flow

Reynolds Number

For a good introduction to the concept of Reynolds number, see Ascher H. Shapiro, *Shape and*

Flow (New York: Anchor Books, 1961). A more comprehensive treatment is the excellent book by G. K. Batchelor, *Introduction to Fluid Dynamics* (New York: Cambridge University Press, 1967). Reynolds's original work appears in Osborne Reynolds, "An Experimental Investigation of the Circumstances Which Determine Whether the Motion of Water Shall Be Direct or Sinuous, and of the Laws of Resistance in Parallel Channels," *Philosophical Transactions of the Royal Society of London,* 174 (1883): 935–982.

Turbulence of the Universe

The role of turbulence in the large-scale universe is set forth in George Gamow, *The Creation of the Universe* (New York: Viking, 1961), as well as in Gamow's articles for the *Scientific American*: "Modern Cosmology," "Turbulence in Space," and "The Evolutionary Universe." The first two articles are reprinted in *The New Astronomy*, a Scientific American book (New York: Simon and Schuster, 1955). For the third article, see *The Universe* (New York: Simon and Schuster, 1956, 1957).

Figure 37*b* is a photograph of the Rosette Nebula in the constellation Monoceros (N6C 2237–9), taken and reproduced by permission of the Harvard College Observatory. Figure 37*d* shows the 36 NGC 6523 nebula in Sagittarius, Messier 8, Lagoon Nebula; 37*f* shows the 5 NGC 1300 barred spiral galaxy in Eridanus; 37*h* shows the 7 NGC 1952 Crab Nebula in Taurus, Messier 1; and 39*a* shows the NGC 5194 spiral galaxy in Canes Venatici, Messier 51, with satellite galaxy NGC 5195.

Vortex Streets

A fine article on whistles and vortex streets is by Robert C. Chanaud, "Aerodynamic Whistles," *Scientific American* 222 (January 1970): 40ff.

The striking photograph of the vortex street in Figure 40 was taken by Owen Griffin and Steven Ramberg of the U.S. Naval Research Laboratory in Washington, D.C., and is reprinted with their permission. See O. M. Griffin and C. W. Votaw, "The Use of Aerosols for the Visualization of Flow Phenomena," *International Journal of Heat Mass Transfer* 16 (Pergamon Press: 1973): 217–219, as well as "The Vortex Street in the Wake of a Vibrating Cylinder," *Journal of Fluid Mechanics* 55 (1972): 31–48.

Heinrich Hertel's outstanding work on swimming snakes, fish propulsion, insect flight, and natural and man-made structures is *Structure, Form and Movement* (New York: Reinhold, 1966).

For a recent study on the vee formation of birds, see P. B. S. Lissaman, and Carl A. Shollenberger, "Formation Flight of Birds," *Science* 168 (22 May 1970): 1003–1005.

Stress and Flow

Feynman's illuminating discussion of the "underlying unity of nature" is in Richard P. Feynman, Robert B. Leighton, and Matthew Sands, *The Feynman Lectures on Physics*, vol. 2, p. 12 (Reading, Mass.: Addison-Wesley, 1964).

Stress in Wood and Bone

The pattern of stress in a beam shown in Figure 47 is redrawn from S. Timoshenko and Gleason H. MacCullough, *Elements of Strength of Materials* (Princeton, N. J.: Van Nostrand, 1949).

An excellent summary of the trajectory theory of stress in the development of bone can be found in Patrick D. F. Murray, *Bones* (Cambridge: At the University Press, 1936). Figure 48 was redrawn from p. 102 of that book. The Thompson reference cited for Figure 72 is, of course, D'Arcy Thompson, *On Growth and Form*, 2nd ed., (Cambridge: At the University Press, 1942). Another good treatment of the growth of bone is Andrew C. Bassett, "Electrical Effects in Bone," *Scientific American* 213 (October 1965): 18–25.

For a review of the little that is known about the effects of electrical currents on the growth of plants, see Bruce I. H. Scott, "Electricity in Plants," *Scientific American* 207 (October 1962): 107–117.

Figure 43, which shows lines of electrical force, is taken from Clerk Maxwell, *A Treatise on Electricity and Magnetism*, vol. 1, Figure 12 (Oxford: Clarendon Press, 1892).

Stress, Flow, and Engineering

A good discussion of the design of architectural shells and the relations between aesthetics and engineering is Curt Siegel, *Structure and Form in Modern Architecture* (New York: Reinhold, 1962).

The Hortonspheroid storage tanks shown in Figure 53*a* were constructed by the Chicago Bridge and Iron Company. They are used for the storage of volatile liquids such as gasoline. The photograph of the drop of water in Figure 53*b* was taken by Dr. Rolf Schaal of Zurich, Switzerland, and is reproduced with his permission.

4
Spirals, Meanders, and Explosions

Spirals

The West Texas quote about the whirligig wind is from a story by Frank Neff and William Henry in B. A. Botkin, editor, *Folk-Say: A Regional Miscellany* (Norman, Oklahoma: University of Oklahoma Press, 1930).

A marvelous book about spirals, especially their right- and left-handedness, is Martin Gardner's *The Ambidextrous Universe* (New York: Basic Books, 1964).

Environmental effects on the coiling of shells are discussed by Stephen J. Gould in "Ecology and Functional Significance of Uncoiling in *Vermicularia spirata*: An Essay on Gastropod Form," *Bulletin of Marine Science* 19 (June 1960): 432–445.

The evolutionary development of the feeding habits of the *Dictyodora*, from random movements to a spiral and then to a helix, are described in Adolf Seilacher, "Fossil Behavior," *Scientific American* 216 (August 1967): 72–80.

For more about the spiraling of shells and horns, see D'Arcy Thompson, *On Growth and Form*, 2nd ed. (Cambridge: At the University Press, 1942).

The photograph of the mountain sheep in Figure 62 is reproduced through the courtesy of L. L. Rue Enterprises of Blairstown, New Jersey.

Meanders

The photograph of the flexible column in Figure 66 is reproduced with the permission of Frei Otto of the Atelier Warmbronn, Warmbronn, Germany.

The photograph of the magnetic domains in garnet shown in Figure 67*b* is reproduced with the permission of Dr. Andrew H. Bobeck of the Bell Telephone Laboratories.

Luna Leopold has written a good deal about river meanders. See Luna Leopold and W. B. Langbein, "River Meanders," *Scientific American* 214 (June 1966): 60–70; for further references, see the more comprehensive Luna B. Leopold, M. G. Wolman and John P. Miller, *Fluvial Processes* in

Geomorphology (San Francisco: Freeman, 1964). Also see Luna B. Leopold and M. Gordan Wolman, "River Meanders," *Bulletin of the Geological Society of America* 71 (1960): 769–794.

Albert Einstein's essay on river meanders is "The Cause of the Formation of Meanders in the Courses of Rivers and of the So-Called Beer's Law" in *Essays in Science* (New York: Wisdom Library, 1933, 1934).

The photograph of the Alaskan river in Figure 69 is reproduced through the courtesy of Georg Gerster.

The movement of snakes is nicely described by Carl Gans, "Locomotion without Limbs," *Natural History* 75 (February 1966): 10–16; and "How Snakes Move," *Scientific American* 222 (June 1970) 82–96.

Explosions

The photograph of the crater Tycho in Figure 72 was taken by the Lick Observatory and is reproduced with its permission.

The handsome photograph of the milk splash in Figure 79 is reproduced with the permission of Dr. Harold E. Edgerton of the Massachusetts Institute of Technology.

A comparison of the growth of ink spots with the growth of biological forms is contained in Paul Weiss, *Principles of Development* (New York: Henry Holt, 1939).

5
Models of Branching

Important papers in the analysis of branching networks, especially streams, include:

Luna B. Leopold and W. B. Langbein, "The Concept of Entropy in Landscape Evolution," *U.S. Geological Survey, Professional Paper* 500A, A1–A20, 1962.

Robert E. Horton, "Erosional Development of Streams and Their Drainage Basins: Hydrophysical Approach to Quantitative Morphology," *Bulletin of the Geological Society of America* 56 (1945): 275–370.

A. N. Strahler, "Hypsometric (Area-Altitude) Analysis of Erosional Topology," *Bulletin of the Geological Society of America* 63 (1952): 1117–1142.

Michael J. Woldenberg, "A Structural Taxonomy of Spatial Hierarchies," *Colston Papers*, vol. 22 (London: Buttersworths Scientific Publishers, 1970); and "Spatial Order in Fluvial Systems: Horton's Laws Derived from Mixed Hexagonal Hierarchies of Drainage Basin Areas," *Bulletin of the Geological Society of America* 80 (1969): 97–111.

Ronald L. Shreve, "Statistical Law of Stream Numbers," *Journal of Geology* 74 (1966): 17–37.

The lightning stroke from which Figure 90 is drawn was originally photographed by Ed Holbert and appeared, by courtesy of Thompson Lightning Protection Inc., in the book *Time* (New York: Time-Life Books, 1966), p. 117.

Least Work and Angles of Branching

Cecil D. Murray's work on the branching angles of arteries and trees is contained in "The Physiological Principle of Minimum Work Applied to the Angle of Branching of Arteries," *Journal of General Physiology* 9 (1926): 835–841; and "A Relationship between Circumference and Weight in Trees and its Bearing on Branching Angles," *Journal of General Physiology* 10 (1927): 725–739.

D'Arcy Thompson discusses Murray's work as well as the observations of W. Roux in *On Growth and Form*, 2nd ed. (Cambridge: At the University Press, 1942), pp. 948–957.

The two quotations by Leonardo da Vinci can be found in Edward MacCurdy, *The Notebooks of Leonardo da Vinci* (New York: Braziller, 1955), pp. 299 and 306.

Trees from Rules

For Ulam's work, see Stanislaw Ulam, "Patterns of Growth of Figures: Mathematical Aspects," in Gyorgy Kepes, editor, *Module, Proportion, Symmetry, Rhythm* (New York: Braziller, 1966), pp. 64–74.

6

Trees

The Plumbing of Trees

See, for example, Martin H. Zimmermann, "How Sap Moves in Trees," *Scientific American* 208, 3 (March 1963).

Evolution of Trees

A short discussion of evolution is contained in E. J. H. Corner, *The Life of Plants* (New York: World Publishing Co., 1964), from which Figure 112 is reproduced.

Klee's drawing of leaves is from Paul Klee, *The Thinking Eye,* edited by Jürg Spiller (New York: George Wittenborn, 1961).

For remarks about the *Xanthorrhea, Welwitschia,* and other exotic trees, see Edwin A. Menninger, *Fantastic Trees* (New York: Viking, 1967).

Basic Patterns of Growth

For an excellent description of the growth of palms, see E. J. H. Corner, *The Natural History of Palms* (Berkeley: University of California Press, 1966).

Le Corbusier's sketch, in slightly modified form, is from F. Le Lionnais, editor, *Great Currents of Mathematical Thought*, vol. 2, p. 178 (New York: Dover, 1971).

Spiral Phyllotaxis

Two very good articles on phyllotaxis are F. J. Richards, "The Geometry of Phyllotaxis and its Origin," in *Growth in Relation to Differentiation and Morphogenesis*, Symposium of the Society for Experimental Biology, No. 2 (New York: Academic Press, 1948); and R. Snow, "Problems of Phyllotaxis and Leaf Determination," *Endeavor*, October 1955, p. 190.

Daniel T. O'Connell described his giant sunflower in a letter to the editor, *Scientific Monthly* 73, 5 (November 1951).

7

Soap Bubbles

The best and most readily available book on soap bubbles is by C. V. Boys, *Soap-Bubbles, Their Colours and the Forces Which Mold Them* (New York: Dover, 1911/1959).

The classic work is, of course, J. A. F. Plateau, *Statique Expérimentale et Théorique des Liquides* (Paris: Gauthier-Villars, 1873).

For further discussion of experiments with thumbtack sandwiches, see Richard Courant and Herbert Robbins, *What is Mathematics?* (New York: Oxford University Press, 1941), 386–397. A very sophisticated sandwich is described in Frei Otto, *Information of the Institute for Lightweight Structures* (IL–1) (University of Stuttgart, 1969, distributed by George Wittenborn, New York).

The crystal micrograph in Figure 150 is Al_2O_3. That micrograph and the micrograph in Figure 151 are reproduced through the courtesy of Dr. Kent Bowen of the Massachusetts Institute of Technology.

Excellent material on the mathematics of bubbles can be found in D'Arcy Thompson, *On Growth and Form*, 2nd ed., (Cambridge: At the University Press, 1942).

Lord Kelvin's work regarding froth is in Sir William Thompson, "On the Division of Space with Minimum Partitional Area," *Philosophical Magazine* 24, 5 (December 1887): 503–514. Matzke's bubble counts can be found in Edwin B. Matzke, "The Three-Dimensional Shape of Bubbles in Foam," *American Journal of Botany* 33,58 (1946).

The quotation from Fuller regarding the incommensurability of pi is from R. Buckminster Fuller, "Conceptuality of Fundamental Structures," in Gyorgy Kepes, editor, *Structure in Art and Science* (New York: Braziller, 1965), p. 71.

We can derive the properties of the average cell in a froth as follows: to determine the number of edges n of the polygon with face angles of $109.47°$, divide the polygon into triangles by drawing lines from its center to each corner. Then, the sum of the angles in the triangles less the face angles of the polygon equals the $360°$ angle at the center; i.e., $180n - 109.47n = 360$. Consequently n, the number of edges, is 5.104. Applying Descartes' rule that the number of degrees at a polyhedral corner equals the amount the face angles at the corner differ from flatness or $360°$, we find that $720/c = 360 - A$, where 720 is the number of degrees in a sphere, and A is the sum of the face angles at a corner ($3 \times 109.47°$). Solving for c, the number of corners of the polyhedron, we get 22.789. Next we apply Euler's formula that the corners c, less the edges e, plus the faces f, equals 2, i.e., $c - e + f = 2$. Knowing that each edge connects two faces, we can write $22.789 - 5.104f/2 + f = 2$, so that the number of faces f equals 13.394. Consequently, as described in the text, the average cell of a froth has 22.789 corners and 13.394 faces with 5.104 edges.

8

Packing and Cracking

A more complete discussion of the phenomena of packing, cracking, and surface tension is "The Forms of Tissues or Cell-Aggregates," chapter 7, in D'Arcy Thompson, *On Growth and Form*, 2nd ed. (Cambridge: At the University Press, 1942).

For an excellent introduction to unit cells and other elementary aspects of crystallography, see the programmed course of instruction by Bruce Chalmers, James G. Holland, Kenneth A. Jackson, and Brady R. Williamson, *Crystallography: A Programmed Course in Three Dimensions* (New York: Meredith Publishing Co., 1965).

The triradiate pattern of gelatin on a shrinking balloon is described by A. J. Bull in *Geological Magazine* 69 (1932): 73–75. The same pattern in the human brain is described in the first article by Le Gros Clark in W. E. Le Gros Clark and P. B. Medawar, editors, *Essays on Growth and Form* (New York: Oxford University Press, 1945).

Wegener's description of continental drift has been reprinted in Alfred Wegener, *The Origin of Continents and Oceans* (New York: Dover, 1966). For more information about sea-floor spreading, see Robert S. Dietz and John C. Holden, "The Breakup of Pangea," *Scientific American*, October 1970, 223, 30–41.

An interesting book on the markings of animals is Adolf Portmann's *Animal Forms and Patterns: A Study of the Appearance of Animals* (Schocken Books, New York, 1967).

Index

MORE ABOUT PENGUINS
AND PELICANS

Penguinews, which appears every month, contains details of all the new books issued by Penguins as they are published. From time to time it is supplemented by *Penguins in Print*, which is our complete list of almost 5,000 titles.

A specimen copy of *Penguinews* will be sent to you free on request. Please write to Dept EP, Penguin Books Ltd, Harmondsworth, Middlesex, for your copy.

In the U.S.A.: For a complete list of books available from Penguins in the United States write to Dept CS, Penguin Books, 625 Madison Avenue, New York, New York 10022.

In Canada: For a complete list of books available from Penguins in Canada write to Penguin Books Canada Ltd, 2801 John Street, Markham, Ontario L3R 1B4.

A Pelican Book

G. E. FOGG

THE GROWTH OF PLANTS

Second Edition – Revised

In a sense man and the animals are parasites on the vegetable world. Ultimately human survival depends and is likely always to depend on plant growth. This book, therefore, by a professor of botany, literally goes to the roots of human existence.

Traditional methods of agriculture may have served us in the past, but the sensational increase in the world's population makes it certain that every resource of botanical science will soon have to be mobilized if we are to avoid disaster.

Outlining what we know today about the general behaviour of plants as they grow, the author explains photosynthesis – with its dependence on chlorophyll – and other processes; the organization of matter into protoplasm, cells, and tissues; the correlations of growth; the formation of roots, leaves, and flowers; the relations between plants and their surroundings, and the rhythms of growth and flowering.

'A large range of readers are going to benefit from this Pelican ... from all view-points in terms of value it rates as a "best-buy" and deserves to be a best-seller' – *Institute of Biology*

PEREGRINE BOOKS

Published at the same time as *Patterns in Nature*

A Modern Herbal   Mrs M. Grieve

First published in 1931, *A Modern Herbal* was the first comprehensive work on herbs in English since Culpepper's work in the
seventeenth century. It provides detailed information on the
chemical and medicinal properties of all herbs to be found in the
British Isles, as well as many from overseas.

Punishment: the Supposed Justifications   Ted Honderich

Bringing rigorous logic to the science of penology, Ted Honderich
examines the doctrines brought forward to justify our practice of
punishing criminals and questions the whole basis of our legal
system.

The Historical Novel   Georg Lukács

In a classic of critical writing, Georg Lukács examines the relationship between past and present in literature, discussing the works of
Sir Walter Scott, Flaubert, Manzoni, Pushkin and Victor Hugo.

'No one interested in the imaginative approach to history should
miss this absorbing study, which will lead him to fresh consideration of such giants as Goethe, Flaubert, Balzac, Tolstoy and even
Shakespeare' – C. V. Wedgewood in the *Daily Telegraph*

Also published:

FICTIONS: THE NOVEL AND SOCIAL REALITY
Michel Zeraffa

United Kingdom £3.50

Science: Ge
ISBN 055.

Cover photograph by Tony Evans

A Peregrine Book
published by Penguin Books